THE KINGFISHER
YOUNG PEOPLE'S BOOK OF
MUSIC

THE KINGFISHER
YOUNG PEOPLE'S BOOK OF
MUSIC

KING*f*ISHER

NEW YORK

Editor: Clive Wilson
Authors: Nicky Barber, Mark Barratt,
Alan Blackwood, Elinor Kelly, Chris de Souza
Consultant: Avril Thompson
Designer: Tracy Killick
Cover Design: Mike Davis
Cover Photograph: Tim Ridley
Index: Stuart Dunlop and Kay Wright
Researcher: Laura Sheppard
Picture Research: Elaine Willis, Su Alexander,
Image Select (London)

KINGFISHER
Larousse Kingfisher Chambers Inc.
95 Madison Avenue
New York, New York 10016

First published in hardcover in 1996
First published in paperback in 1999
4 6 8 10 9 7 5 3 (HC)
(HC)-2TR/0699/TWP/NEW/GPM115
2 4 6 8 10 9 7 5 3 1 (PB)
(PB)-1TR/0699/TWP/NEW/GPM115

LIBRARY OF CONGRESS CATALOGING-IN-PUBLICATION DATA
The Kingfisher young people's book of music.—
1st American ed. 1996
p. cm.
Discography: p.
Includes bibliographical references and index.
Summary: An authoritative introduction to musical periods
and styles from ancient times to the present day
1. Music—History and criticism—Juvenile literature.
[1. Music]
ML3928.K54 1996
780'.9—dc20 96-3532 CIP AC MN

ISBN 1-85697-586-X (HC)
ISBN 0-7534-5250-2 (PB)
Printed in Singapore

Contents

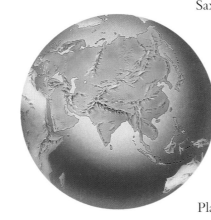

How to Use This Book

The Kingfisher Young People's Book of Music has many features to help you explore the fascinating world of music. Time lines show what was happening in the arts, sciences, history, and music during a particular period. Mini globes pinpoint the location of different musical traditions across the world and listening guides highlight essential musical pieces. The feature spreads themselves give an insider's view on four fascinating subjects—Indian classical dance, buildings for music, the life and times of Ludwig van Beethoven, and the musical, West Side Story. At the back you will find a reference section. This includes a glossary that explains many of the terms used in the book. These two pages show you how to get the most out of The Kingfisher Young People's Book of Music.

Music notation appears throughout the book. To find out more about these symbols see the *Music to the Ears* chapter and the *Glossary*.

A historical picture introduces the main topic covered by the spread. It appears in the top left-hand corner of each page.

The main text examines fascinating topics from almost every area of music.

Illustrated boxes contain additional in-depth information related to the topic.

The time line runs throughout the chapter called *Music in Time and Place*. It tells you, at a glance, important achievements in music, the arts, sciences, and exploration and major historical events that took place during the period covered.

Symbols identify each event in the time line:
- ♪ Music
- ☛ Historical events
- ♀ Science and exploration
- ♚ The Arts

MUSIC IN TIME AND PLACE

The Middle Ages

The Middle Ages span almost a thousand years of European history. They began with the breakup of the western Roman Empire in the A.D. 470s, and ended in the 1400s, when some of the countries we know today were beginning to take shape. In the early Middle Ages, the Christian church began to develop a type of music known as Gregorian chant, or plainsong. Based on ancient Jewish chanting, this music was sung in unison and without any accompanying instruments.

In around A.D. 1000, Guido d'Arezzo, a Benedictine monk, invented staff notation. This way of writing down music had a major impact on the way music was sung. Western music moved away from its Middle Eastern origins and developed harmony, which is writing two or more notes to be played together in the form of chords. In the mid–1300s, Guillaume de Machaut was celebrated for the harmonies and beauty of his music. For the first time, composers were recognized as artists with their own individual styles.

△ In this illuminated manuscript from the 1070s, King David plucks a harp. Below him a minstrel plays a rebec, an early ancestor of the violin.

△ Guido d'Arezzo, shown here on the left, invented staff notation. This way of writing down notes is still used today.

▽ "Summer is coming in," an English song composed around 1310, celebrates the end of winter. The words are written in English and Latin.

WANDERING MUSICIANS

Outside the Church, a whole range of secular (nonreligious) music was performed during the Middle Ages. From about A.D. 1000 students known as Goliards began to wander from court to court across Europe reciting poetry and songs. Jongleurs were traveling performers who entertained audiences in towns and villages with music, juggling, and acrobatic feats. During the late 1100s and 1200s, poet-musicians called troubadours sang tales of courtly love and chivalry. Many troubadours were knights and noblemen.

◁ In the Middle Ages, Christians believed that the end of the world would be heralded by angels blowing trumpets. This picture was painted in Germany during the 1400s.

TIME LINE
- ☛ A.D. 476 End of the Roman Empire in Europe
- ♪ 590–600 Gregory I makes collection of plainsong
- ♚ 698 Lindisfarne Gospel, produced in England
- ♪ 750s Wind organs first developed
- ☛ 800 Charlemagne becomes first Holy Roman Emperor
- ♚ 800s Romanesque style of architecture emerges in Europe
- ♪ c. 1000 Guido d'Arezzo invents staff notation
- ☛ 1066 William of Normandy becomes King of England
- ♪ 1120s Rise of troubadours in France
- ♪ 1150 Notre Dame School of Music is founded
- ♚ 1230 Gothic cathedral of Chartres, France, is completed
- ♪ c. 1250 Motet form of singing develops
- ♀ 1276 First paper mill built, in Italy
- ♀ 1350 Clavichord, an early keyboard instrument, invented
- ♚ 1386–1400 Chaucer's *Canterbury Tales* written

34

35

Labels help pinpoint the main details on the larger images.

Side panels illustrate one special aspect of the feature spreads.

The feature spreads take an in-depth look at particular subjects. You can identify them by their pale blue pages and large, detailed illustrations.

Listen for panels highlight some of the best-known pieces of music associated with particular instruments.

Color photographs and illustrations bring the featured subject vividly to life.

Exploded illustrations in the *Instruments* chapter show the parts that make up the instrument and how the pieces fit together.

Captions give details about the illustrations and photographs.

Pitch and position boxes show where an instrument is played in the orchestra. They also show the relative sizes of instruments from the same family, as well as the highest and lowest notes that each one can play.

Famous musicians are shown playing their instruments throughout the *Instruments* chapter.

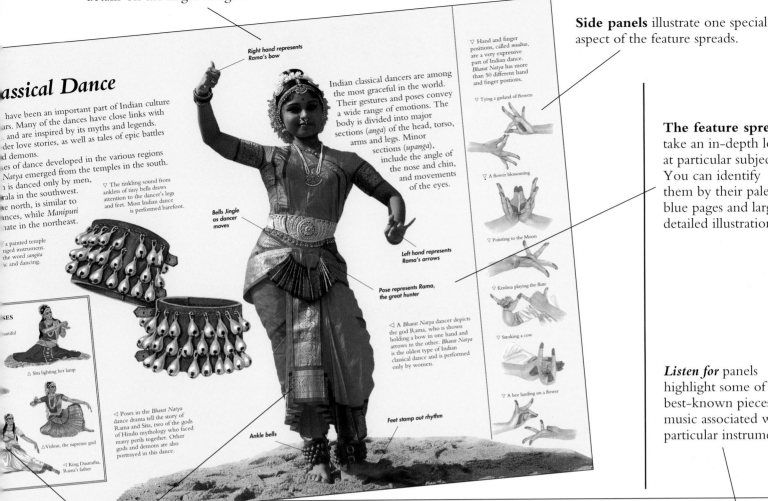

assical Dance

have been an important part of Indian culture
rs. Many of the dances have close links with
and are inspired by its myths and legends.
der love stories, as well as tales of epic battles
d demons.
es of dance developed in the various regions
Natya emerged from the temples in the south.
is danced only by men,
ala in the southwest.
e north, is similar to
ances, while *Manipuri*
ate in the northeast.
a painted temple
nged instrument.
the word *sangita*
ic and dancing.

Indian classical dancers are among the most graceful in the world. Their gestures and poses convey a wide range of emotions. The body is divided into major sections (*anga*) of the head, torso, arms and legs. Minor sections (*upanga*), include the angle of the nose and chin, and movements of the eyes.

Right hand represents Rama's bow

▽ The tinkling sound from anklets of tiny bells draws attention to the dancer's legs and feet. Most Indian dance is performed barefoot.

Bells jingle as dancer moves

Left hand represents Rama's arrows

Pose represents Rama, the great hunter

◁ A *Bharat Natya* dancer depicts the god Rama, who is shown holding a bow in one hand and arrows in the other. *Bharat Natya* is the oldest type of Indian classical dance and is performed only by women.

◁ Poses in the *Bharat Natya* dance drama tell the story of Rama and Sita, two of the gods of Hindu mythology who faced many perils together. Other gods and demons are also portrayed in this dance.

Ankle bells

Feet stamp out rhythm

ES

eautiful

△ Sita lighting her lamp

△ Vishnu, the supreme god

◁ King Dasaratha, Rama's father

▽ Hand and finger positions, called *mudras*, are a very expressive part of Indian dance. *Bharat Natya* has more than 50 different hand and finger positions.

▽ Tying a garland of flowers

▽ A flower blossoming

▽ Pointing to the Moon

▽ Krishna playing the flute

▽ Stroking a cow

▽ A bee landing on a flower

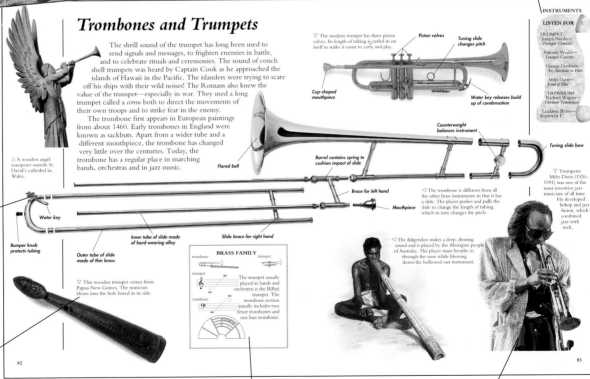

Trombones and Trumpets

The shrill sound of the trumpet has long been used to send signals and messages, to frighten enemies in battle, and to celebrate rituals and ceremonies. The sound of conch shell trumpets was heard by Captain Cook as he approached the islands of Hawaii in the Pacific. The islanders were trying to scare off his ships with their wild noises! The Romans also knew the value of the trumpet—especially in war. They used a long trumpet called a *cornu* both to direct the movements of their own troops and to strike fear in the enemy.

The trombone first appears in European paintings from about 1460. Early trombones in England were known as sackbuts. Apart from a wider tube and a different mouthpiece, the trombone has changed very little over the centuries. Today, the trombone has a regular place in marching bands, orchestras and in jazz music.

△ A wooden angel trumpeter outside St. David's cathedral in, Wales.

Water key

Bumper knob protects tubing

Outer tube of slide made of thin brass

Inner tube of slide made of hard-wearing alloy

Slide brace for right hand

▽ This wooden trumpet comes from Papua New Guinea. The musician blows into the hole bored in its side.

▽ The modern trumpet has three piston valves. Its length of tubing is curled in on itself to make it easier to carry and play.

Piston valves

Tuning slide changes pitch

Cup-shaped mouthpiece

Water key releases build up of condensation

Counterweight balances instrument

Flared bell

Barrel contains spring to cushion impact of slide

Tuning slide bow

Brace for left hand

Mouthpiece

◁ The trombone is different from all the other brass instruments in that it has a slide. The player pushes and pulls the slide to change the length of tubing, which in turn changes the pitch.

BRASS FAMILY

trombone — trumpet

The trumpet usually played in bands and orchestras is the B(flat) trumpet. The trombone section usually includes two tenor trombones and one bass trombone.

◁ The didgeridoo makes a deep, droning sound and is played by the Aborigine people of Australia. The player must breathe in through the nose while blowing down the hollowed out instrument.

▽ Trumpeter Miles Davis (1926–1991) was one of the most inventive jazz musicians of all time. He developed bebop and jazz fusion, which combined jazz with rock.

INSTRUMENTS

LISTEN FOR

TRUMPET
Joseph Haydn—
Trumpet Concerto

Antonio Vivaldi—
Trumpet Concerto

George Gershwin—
An American in Paris

Miles Davis—
Kind of Blue

TROMBONE
Richard Wagner—
Overture Tannhäuser

Luciano Berio—
Sequenza V

82

83

A World of Music

▽ Jazz has its roots in the southern part of North America. You can read about this explosive mixture of African rhythms and European harmony on pages 50–51. Discover the musical heritage of Native Americans on pages 30–31.

▷ Classical music in Europe has a long and fascinating history. Its story is told on pages 34–49.

▷ The catchy rhythms of Latin American music have conquered the world of dancing. Much older still are the panpipes, which have been played in South America for thousands of years. To find out more turn to pages 28–29.

▷ Africa has an amazing range of instruments, including many made from gourds, or dried vegetables. To read about these and other fascinating instruments from around the world turn to pages 58–89.

All over the world, people play and listen to music. There are as many kinds of music as there are peoples and places. In every corner of the globe, music plays an important part: in people's lives, in religious worship, as entertainment, as a means of communication, or simply as an enjoyable pastime.

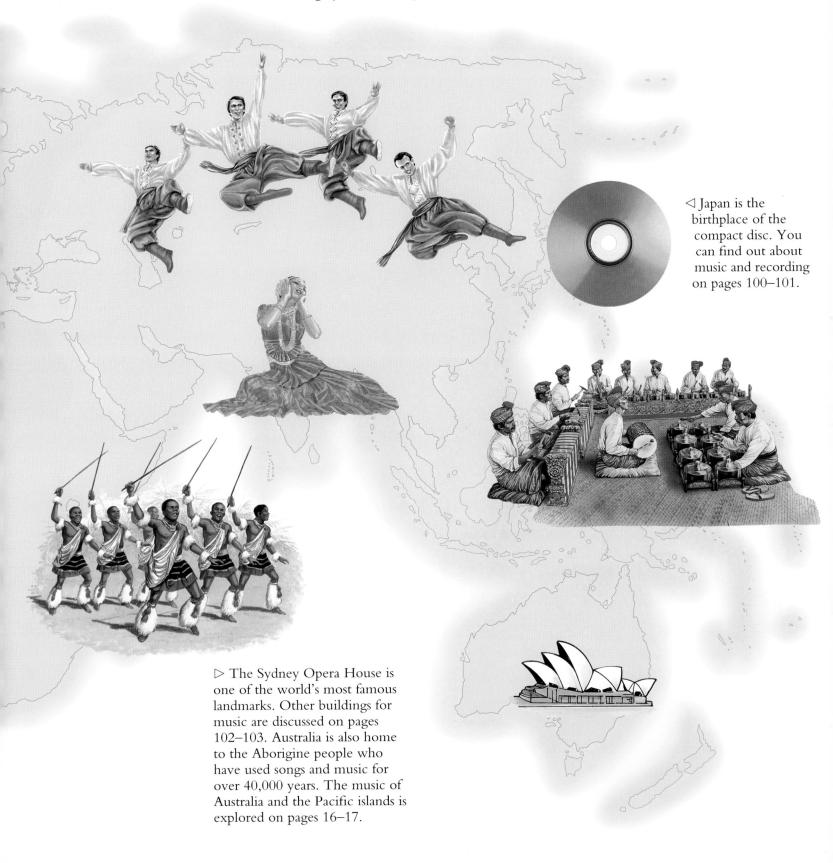

◁ Japan is the birthplace of the compact disc. You can find out about music and recording on pages 100–101.

▷ The Sydney Opera House is one of the world's most famous landmarks. Other buildings for music are discussed on pages 102–103. Australia is also home to the Aborigine people who have used songs and music for over 40,000 years. The music of Australia and the Pacific islands is explored on pages 16–17.

Sounds and Notes

Sound is energy in the form of vibrations called soundwaves. A plucked string, for example, starts the air vibrating. Our eardrums pick up the movements, and our brain interprets them as sounds. A musical note is made when a vibration is steady.

Notes can be organized in scales running from low to high. Different scales have been used at different times in history and vary enormously around the world. Western scales have eight notes. Each set of eight notes is called an octave. Scales made up of five notes are used in Chinese, Celtic, Inuit, and African music. Notes are separated by "intervals." An "interval" is the distance in pitch between one note and another. Intervals vary around the world. The "quivering" feel to some Indian or Chinese music is because the interval between each note is very tiny. The notes of Indian scales are arranged in traditional patterns called *ragas,* which represent different emotions and moods.

Musical sounds can be long or short, loud or quiet. They also vary in "tone." This is the quality that makes our voices and instruments sound different from each other.

△ A medieval manuscript showing the philosophers Pythagoras *(top right)* and Boethius *(top left).* Through experiments and theory, they laid the foundations for today's system of notes and scales.

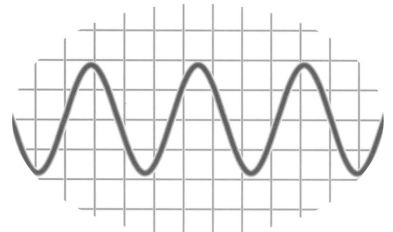

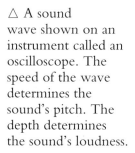

△ A sound wave shown on an instrument called an oscilloscope. The speed of the wave determines the sound's pitch. The depth determines the sound's loudness.

▷ A scale is a number of notes, ascending or descending in "steps." There is a fixed interval between each step. The Western scale is made up of eight notes, seven of which are named A to G. The eighth, or finishing note, has the same letter as the starting note. Here the scale of C is shown.

Treble clef

Middle C in the treble clef **C** **D**

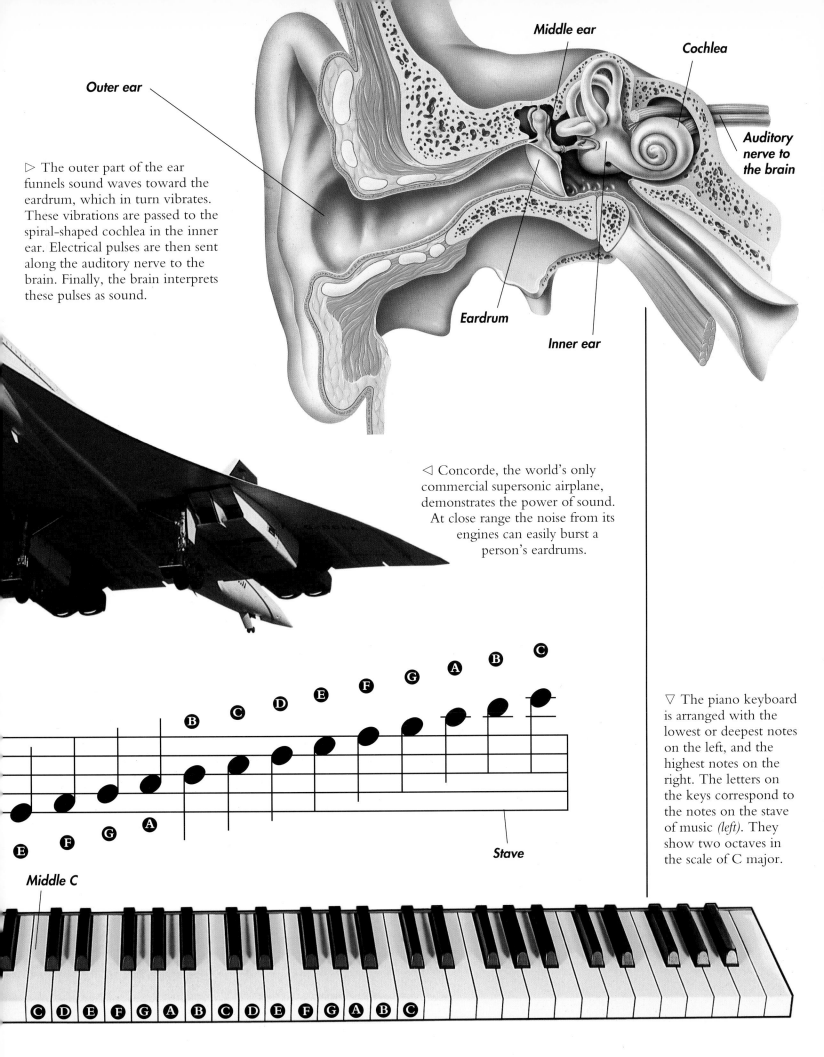

Middle ear

Cochlea

Outer ear

Auditory
nerve to
the brain

▷ The outer part of the ear
funnels sound waves toward the
eardrum, which in turn vibrates.
These vibrations are passed to the
spiral-shaped cochlea in the inner
ear. Electrical pulses are then sent
along the auditory nerve to the
brain. Finally, the brain interprets
these pulses as sound.

Eardrum

Inner ear

◁ Concorde, the world's only
commercial supersonic airplane,
demonstrates the power of sound.
At close range the noise from its
engines can easily burst a
person's eardrums.

▽ The piano keyboard
is arranged with the
lowest or deepest notes
on the left, and the
highest notes on the
right. The letters on
the keys correspond to
the notes on the stave
of music *(left)*. They
show two octaves in
the scale of C major.

Stave

Middle C

Music's Heartbeat

Music without rhythm would be like a person without a backbone. It would collapse in a heap. Rhythm is nearly always a regular pulse or beat, usually easy to tap the foot to, or to dance to. Like the ticking of a clock, it marks the passage of time.

This rhythmic pulse or beat is measured in regular sections called bars. Various types of music have their own number of beats to the bar. This is written down in two numbers at the beginning of the piece of music and is called the time signature. The top number tells you how many beats are in each bar. The bottom one shows you how long each beat lasts. The waltz has three beats to the bar, while most rock music has four beats to the bar.

△ The beating of drums is one of the oldest and most wide-spread forms of music. These Persian women are dancing to the rhythmic sound of the drums.

Different countries and cultures have their own rhythms. African music has complex rhythms created by mixing a variety of drum and bell beats or hand-clapping. African rhythms combined with American band traditions and European harmonies form the basis for jazz. Native American music generally has two separate rhythms, one for the drums and one for vocals.

▷ The North African Berbers make use of hand-clapping as well as drums. Clapping to a beat expresses our feeling for rhythm in the most natural way.

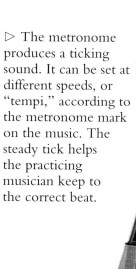

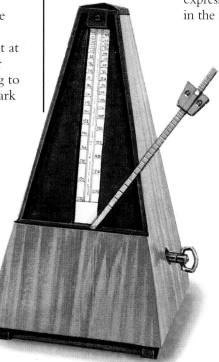

▷ The metronome produces a ticking sound. It can be set at different speeds, or "tempi," according to the metronome mark on the music. The steady tick helps the practicing musician keep to the correct beat.

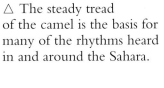

△ The steady tread
of the camel is the basis for
many of the rhythms heard
in and around the Sahara.

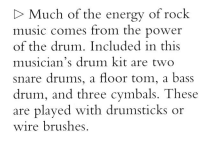

▷ Much of the energy of rock
music comes from the power
of the drum. Included in this
musician's drum kit are two
snare drums, a floor tom, a bass
drum, and three cymbals. These
are played with drumsticks or
wire brushes.

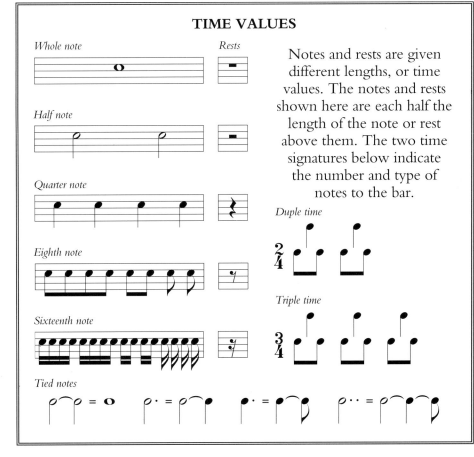

TIME VALUES

Notes and rests are given
different lengths, or time
values. The notes and rests
shown here are each half the
length of the note or rest
above them. The two time
signatures below indicate
the number and type of
notes to the bar.

Whole note

Rests

Half note

Quarter note

Eighth note

Sixteenth note

Tied notes

Duple time

Triple time

Writing Music Down

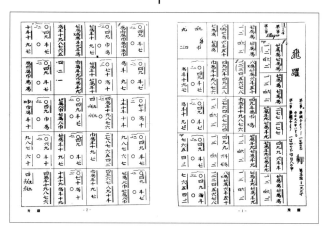

△ Japanese *koto* music uses the *Ikuta* system of notation. Reading down each column indicates which strings are to be played as well as the basic beat.

Most cultures have developed their own musical systems. Not all, however, place great importance on writing music down. Much non-Western music —as well as some Western music—is passed from person to person simply by being listened to and repeated. This can make music feel alive and vibrant. It can also, unfortunately, lead to the loss of very beautiful pieces.

The most-widely used method of writing music is Western notation. Notes are written on a set of five lines, called a stave, and placed higher or lower according to their pitch. By describing the length of each note or rest, it also shows rhythm. Other words or signs tell the musician whether he or she should play loudly or softly, lively or smoothly.

Each piece of music has a shape. Just like a story, the composer gives it a beginning, a middle, and an end. Written music draws our attention to this structure, showing how basic tunes or rhythms are repeated or developed.

△ Jazz musicians improvising. Despite notation, a good deal of music has always been improvised— that is, made up on the spur of the moment. The musicians start with a tune or rhythm, developing it as the mood builds up.

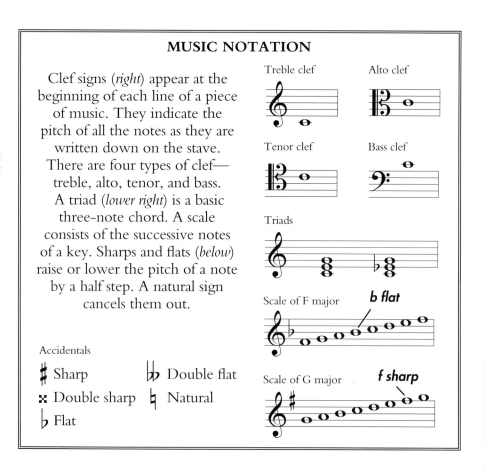

MUSIC NOTATION

Clef signs (*right*) appear at the beginning of each line of a piece of music. They indicate the pitch of all the notes as they are written down on the stave. There are four types of clef— treble, alto, tenor, and bass. A triad (*lower right*) is a basic three-note chord. A scale consists of the successive notes of a key. Sharps and flats (*below*) raise or lower the pitch of a note by a half step. A natural sign cancels them out.

Treble clef

Alto clef

Tenor clef

Bass clef

Triads

Scale of F major

b flat

Scale of G major

f sharp

Accidentals

♯ Sharp

𝄪 Double sharp

♭ Flat

♭♭ Double flat

♮ Natural

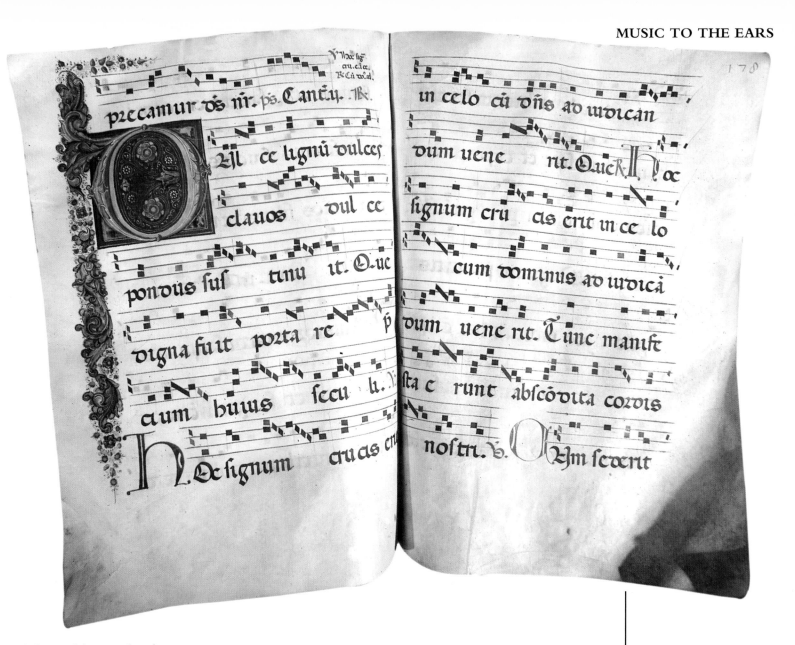

△ A beautiful example of medieval Western notation. The pitched notes of the melody are positioned on the stave and the words of the song written underneath. A more primitive system of "neumes," which reminded the singer of the tune's "shape," existed as early as the 600s.

▷ A range of ideas lies behind every musical performance. The Chinese musical system has as its foundation a single note, or "yellow bell." From this a series of twelve notes was born, linked with the hours of the day and the months of the year.

Oceania and Australia

Scattered across the deep waters of the Pacific Ocean are thousands of islands whose musical traditions are closely bound up with the sea. The people who live in this region, known as Oceania, once traveled from island to island by canoe. They took drums, flutes, and pipes with them and settled on islands such as those of Hawaii and Papua New Guinea. Their music still includes chants to help them navigate.

Thought to be one of the oldest peoples in the world, the Aborigines first came to Australia from Southeast Asia about 50,000 years ago. A great deal of their music relies on the voice and natural sounds such as hand-clapping or foot-stamping. Many of their songs and dances tell how the Earth was created. These rituals, as well as their musical instruments, have probably not changed much in tens of thousands of years.

△ Music, singing, and dancing have always been central to the Aborigine's way of life. This cave painting shows figures playing the didgeridoo and performing a ceremonial dance.

△ At a ceremonial dance in Papua New Guinea, the rhythm is maintained by a *kundu* (hourglass) drum. The music of this island includes warlike chanting and yodeling, as well as more gentle flute and drum music.

◁ The didgeridoo is made from tree branches hollowed out by termites. Traditionally only men were allowed to play this sacred Aboriginal instrument.

THE BULL ROARER

The bull roarer has been used for more than 25,000 years by peoples around the world. Usually made of wood and attached to a length of cord, it makes a screaming sound when spun through the air. The decorations on this bull roarer from Papua New Guinea are believed to have magical powers that can drive out evil spirits.

▷ The chants and shouts of the New Zealand Maori war dance, or *haka*, are accompanied by foot-stamping and unusual facial grimaces. Sometimes the warriors stick out their tongues.

◁ Hawaiian singers at a sacred festival beat on drums made from gourds, large dried and hollowed-out fruit or vegetable husks. Their songs are addressed to the gods and may be accompanied by a dance, or *hula*.

▽ The Pacific Ocean covers about one-third of the world's surface. Oceania stretches from the Hawaiian Islands to New Zealand. Australia lies to the west.

Eastern Asia

△ A flute player performing at the Chinese court 500 years ago. Musicians played at festivals, banquets, and on the emperor's birthday.

The musical traditions of this region go back thousands of years. Much of ancient Chinese music was written for court dances and musical theater, while Japan's celebrated *No* plays are an elaborate mixture of theater, music, and dancing. However, instrumental music is no less important. Many solo pieces attempt to evoke particular poetic sensations in the listener, such as the haunting "Autumn Moon in the Han Palace" from China, or "The Distant Sound of the Deer" from Japan.

Music also plays a vital role in religious ceremonies. It has strong links with Shinto, the most ancient religion of Japan. In Thailand music is performed during Buddhist rites and rituals. Percussion instruments of all kinds—drums, gongs, cymbals, and bells—are used to placate the gods or to scare away demons. Perhaps the most remarkable ceremonial music of all is made by the *gamelan* orchestras of Java and Bali. According to legend, the first *gamelan* was created by the ancient gods who spoke to one another by beating gongs and tinkling chimes.

△ The Korean *p'i p'a* is an ancient instument that is plucked. Its orgins go back over 2,000 years. It is also popular in China.

◁ Japanese religious ceremonies often make use of large drums as well as gongs and high-pitched flutes. This enormous drum belongs to a Japanese Shinto temple. Followers of the Shinto religion worship the spirits of their ancestors.

▷ A Buddhist monk in a Tibetan monastery calls his fellow monks to prayer by striking a frame drum. Buddhists chant their prayers.

◁ The *gamelan* orchestras of Java and Bali contain a wide array of different percussion instruments. *Gamelans* are heard at all kinds of occasions, and provide accompaniment to the famous Balinese "shadow plays."

TIME LINE

✍ **c. 2000 B.C.** Chinese Yellow River civilization begins

♪ **c. 1000 B.C.** First mouth organ used in China

✍ **50 B.C.–A.D. 50** Buddhism introduced into China

♪ **c. 100** First *gamelan*-like instruments brought to Java from India

♪ **c. 500** Gongs first used in China

♪ **700s** Japanese court music developed

♪ **1300s** *No* plays first performed in Japan

✍ **1368–1644** Ming emperors rule China

🎭 **c. 1800** Peking Opera developed

✍ **1945** Atomic bomb dropped on Hiroshima in Japan

✍ **1949** Mao Tse-Tung creates People's Republic of China

▽ Eastern and Southeast Asia consists of China, Korea, Japan, Thailand, Vietnam, Malaysia, Laos, Myanmar, Cambodia, Tibet, and the many islands of Indonesia.

India and Its Neighbors

△ Dancers celebrate a wedding in this Indian painting dating back to the 1500s. Their graceful movements are accompanied by tambourines, drums, and wind instruments.

The vast region of the Indian subcontinent is home to many different peoples. Hundreds of musical traditions exist side by side, each with their own songs, dances, and instrumental music. Stringed instruments, such as the *sitar* and the bowed fiddle, are popular in northern India, while a variety of flutes and trumpets are favored in the south.

Indian classical music from the north is based on a complicated series of scales called *ragas*, each one particular to a special mood, time of day, and season. To play this kind of music with its intricate patterns of notes and rhythms requires many years of practice.

The voice is also highly regarded as an instrument, and this region has some of the richest song collections in the world. Most are religious songs inspired by the Hindu, Muslim, and Buddhist faiths. The soaring, expressive melodies of Qawaali music, played in India and Pakistan, are thought to bring both the listener and the performer closer to god.

◁ On the banks of the Ganges River in India, a *tabla* player drums out the rhythm as a *sitar* player performs an intricate scale, or *raga*. There are more than 200 different *ragas* in Indian classical music.

▷ Religious celebrations take place throughout the year in India and the surrounding countries. In Kandy, Sri Lanka, elephants accompanied by dancers and drummers lead a procession in the Kandy Esala Perahera. This ten-day-long festival honors a sacred tooth that is believed to have once belonged to Buddha.

◁ A Hindu singer from Bangladesh performs a traditional love song. A mixture of Asian and Western instruments provides the background for the highly expressive words.

▷ Many of the instruments and folk songs performed in the Muslim country of Pakistan echo its musical traditions as well as those of neighboring India.

TIME LINE

🔫 **c. 3000 B.C.** Indus Valley civilization founded (now Pakistan)

🔫 **c. 563 B.C.** Birth of Buddha

🎭 **c. 400 B.C.** *Mahabharata*, the world's longest poem, is begun

🔫 **273 B.C.** Emperor Asoka rules India and spreads Buddhism

🔫 **A.D. 1000** Muslim invasion of India

♪ **1200s** *Sitar* and *tabla* invented

♪ **1200s** Development of *ragas*

🔫 **1757** Start of British control of India

🔫 **1947** India and Pakistan become independent

🔫 **1948** Sri Lanka wins independence from British rule

▽ As well as the country of India, the Indian subcontinent includes Pakistan in the northwest, Nepal in the north, Bangladesh in the east, and the island of Sri Lanka in the far south.

Indian Classical Dance

Music and dancing have been an important part of Indian culture for thousands of years. Many of the dances have close links with the Hindu religion and are inspired by its myths and legends. These include tender love stories, as well as tales of epic battles between gods and demons.

Different styles of dance developed in the various regions of India. *Bharat Natya* emerged from the temples in the south. *Kathakali*, which is danced only by men, comes from Kerala in the southwest. *Kathak*, from the north, is similar to Muslim court dances, while *Manipuri* folk dances originate in the northeast.

◁ A carved statue of a painted temple dancer holding a stringed instrument. From ancient times the word *sangita* has meant both music and dancing.

▽ The tinkling sound from anklets of tiny bells draws attention to the dancer's legs and feet. Most Indian dance is performed barefoot.

BHARAT NATYA POSES

△ Rama grieving over the loss of Sita

◁ Sita, the beautiful and virtuous

△ Sita lighting her lamp

▽ Rama destroying the demon king, Ravana

△ Ravana, the evil demon king

△ Vishnu, the supreme god

◁ King Dasaratha, Rama's father

◁ Poses in the *Bharat Natya* dance drama tell the story of Rama and Sita, two of the gods of Hindu mythology who faced many perils together. Other gods and demons are also portrayed in this dance.

Right hand represents Rama's bow

Indian classical dancers are among the most graceful in the world. Their gestures and poses convey a wide range of emotions. The body is divided into major sections (*anga*), including the head, torso, arms, and legs. Minor sections (*upanga*) include the angle of the nose and chin and movements of the eyes.

Bells jingle as dancer moves

Left hand represents Rama's arrows

Pose represents Rama, the great hunter

◁ A *Bharat Natya* dancer depicts the god Rama, who is shown holding a bow in one hand and arrows in the other. *Bharat Natya* is the oldest type of Indian classical dance and is performed only by women.

Ankle bells

Feet stamp out rhythm

▽ Hand and finger positions, called *mudras*, are a very expressive part of Indian dance. *Bharat Natya* has more than 50 different hand and finger positions.

▽ Tying a garland of flowers

▽ A flower blossoming

▽ Pointing to the Moon

▽ Krishna playing the flute

▽ Stroking a cow

▽ A bee landing on a flower

The Heart of Africa

The vast area south of the Sahara has a varied landscape of mountains, rivers, forests, and deserts. It contains over forty countries and hundreds of different tribal regions, and is the source of a remarkable number of musical traditions. Common to all are powerful rhythms, beaten out on drums of every type and size. The training a tribal drummer has to undergo is every bit as demanding as that of a Western classical musician, and often begins at an early age. Other instruments—most made from natural materials—also feature prominently in traditional African music. These include zithers and fiddles fashioned from gourds, flutes made of wood, and trumpets carved from ivory and animal horn.

But it is song that lies at the heart of much African music. There are songs to celebrate weddings and births, songs to help deal with sickness and death, and songs to accompany work. Whatever the event—big or small—there is usually some kind of song to mark its passing.

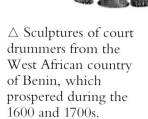

△ Sculptures of court drummers from the West African country of Benin, which prospered during the 1600 and 1700s.

▽ War dances are just one of many dances performed by the Zulu people of South Africa. There is even a Zulu dance for making a complaint to the local chief or king.

▷ Drumming dominates the music of the Yoruba people from Nigeria. The lead drummer of this percussion group is playing on an *iyalu* (mother of the drums), which "talks" by imitating Yoruba speech.

▽ In Zaire, Central Africa, tribal gatherings and dances are always accompanied by the rhythms of the drums. Xylophones, too, are commonly played. Here a spiritual leader prepares to lead a ritual dance.

FOOT DRUMS

African "foot drums" are often carved in human shapes, and are designed to stand on their own two carved feet. Many of these drums have a ritual importance and are used in religious ceremonies. The drum is also used to beat out messages imitating speech—a very good way of communicating in dense jungle or over great stretches of grassland or desert.

▽ Traditional African music comes from countries that include Nigeria and the Sudan all the way south to the South African Republic.

The Middle East

△ The musician in the center of this ancient Sumerian mosaic is playing a lyre, one of the oldest types of instrument and an ancestor of the harp. The Sumerian civilization developed in the land now known as Iraq.

The history of the different lands and peoples that make up the Middle East stretches back over 5,000 years. It was here that the first great civilizations of Sumer, Assyria, Babylon, and Egypt developed. Among their musical legacies were the early ancestors of the modern violin, oboe, and trumpet.

The Middle East was also the birthplace of the Jewish, Christian, and Muslim faiths. The Bible contains many references to music in early Jewish worship, including the chanting of psalms, which was later taken up by Christians. The music of the early Eastern Church developed into the chants and hymns sung in Greek and Russian Orthodox churches today.

After its founding in the A.D. 600s, the Muslim faith—or Islam—quickly spread throughout the Middle East, North Africa, and even into Spain. Intricate rhythms and sound patterns are typical of Muslim music. Singers known as *muezzin* still bring the faithful to prayer five times a day with a call that requires great skill to sing.

△ These Muslim mystics, called dervishes, worship Allah (God) by repeating a prayer and performing a whirling dance that takes them into an ecstatic trance. Many religions still include dance in their ceremonies.

▷ A woman of the wandering Tuareg tribe in North Africa's Sahara Desert coaxes a tune from a one-stringed fiddle. This ancient instrument is often used to accompany songs usually sung by men.

▽ The *shofar*, a wind instrument made from a ram's horn, was used by the Hebrew people in ancient times and is mentioned in the Bible. It can still be heard in synagogues during religious ceremonies.

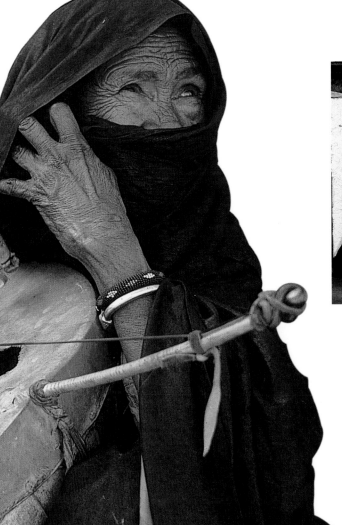

△ The influence of Muslim culture in medieval Spain survives in modern Spanish flamenco dance. The stamping of the dancer's feet, the clicking of castanets, and the accompanying chanted song all originally came from North Africa.

TIME LINE

☞ **c. 3500 B.C.** World's first civilization starts in Sumeria

♪ **c. 3200 B.C.** First harps and flutes made

♀ **c. 2600 B.C.** Building of the first pyramids in Egypt

☻ **332 B.C.** Founding of Alexandria as great cultural center

☞ **c. 1280 B.C.** Birth of Moses

☞ **c.5 B.C.** Birth of Jesus Christ

☞ **A.D. 570** Birth of Muhammad, founder of the Muslim religion

☞ **c. 750–1490** The Moors, a Muslim people from North Africa, occupy Spain

☞ **1948** The state of Israel is created

☞ **1990–1991** Iraq invades Kuwait in Persian Gulf War

▽ Middle Eastern countries include Iran, Iraq, Syria, Saudi Arabia, Israel, and Egypt. North Africa covers Tunisia, Algeria, and Morocco.

Latin America

A series of great empires once thrived in Mexico, and Central and South America. The Mayans, and later the Toltecs, Incas, and Aztecs, made music an important part of their way of life. An Aztec musician who played a wrong note during a religious ceremony could be put to death! Rattles, scrapers, drums, and wind instruments formed the basis of the music made by each of these cultures.

During the 1500s, Spanish and Portuguese settlers and soldiers conquered many of the lands in this region. Some of the older types of music blended with the Spanish and Portuguese songs and dances to create what is known as Latin American music. Its lively rhythm was also influenced by the music African slaves brought with them when they were sent to work on the plantations of the Caribbean. Today, Latin American dance rhythms such as the tango, rumba, bossa nova, and samba are enjoyed all over the world.

△ A Toltec figure made of pottery beats a drum. The Toltecs were a warrior-like people who ruled in Central America from A.D. 900 to 1100.

△ The gentle sound of the panpipes is heard in Bolivia, Peru, Ecuador, and parts of Argentina and Chile. This ancient instrument, known locally as the *antaras* or *zampoñas*, has bamboo pipes.

▽ A hunter from the Amazon rain forest plays a one-stringed bow. Biting hold of one end, he uses his mouth and teeth to resonate the sound and to change pitch.

▷ The harp was introduced to Peru and other parts of South America by early European settlers. Today, it is a popular instrument among the *mestizos*, which is the term used for the mixed race descendants of the native peoples and the European settlers.

▽ The Carnival of Rio de Janeiro, Brazil, is a religious festival celebrated each year during the four days before the Christian period of Lent. It is a riot of color and high spirits as thousands of dancers and musicians throng the streets.

ADOLPH ZUKOR presents
GEORGE RAFT
CAROLE LOMBARD

Rumba

with MARGO · LYNNE OVERMAN · MONROE OWSLEY · IRIS ADRIAN · GAIL PATRICK

△ By the 1930s, Latin American dances such as the Cuban rumba were featuring in Hollywood films. The energetic rhythms could also be heard in dance halls and nightclubs throughout Europe and the United States. Later, the samba and the conga became just as popular.

TIME LINE

♪ **200–100 B.C.** Flutes and panpipes played in the Andes

🎭 **c. A.D. 250** Mayan culture dominates Central America

c. 1300 Creation of the Aztec Empire in Mexico and the Inca Empire in Peru

♀ **1492** Christopher Columbus arrives in the Caribbean islands

1521 Spanish destroy Aztec Empire

1532 Spanish conquer Inca Empire

1600s Slaves brought from Africa to work in the Caribbean

1824 Simón Bolívar ends Spanish rule in much of South America

1959 Fidel Castro becomes Communist leader of Cuba

▽ Latin America includes the whole of South and Central America and the islands of the West Indies.

Native Americans

The musical traditions of Native Americans go back thousands of years. Originally nomads, probably from Asia, these people settled in many parts of the Americas and over time developed their own distinctive customs.

Nevertheless, the music of the different tribes has much in common. Most of it is sung, either by a group or by a solo voice, and it reflects their belief in the spirits of the natural world.

Despite the loss of their land to Europeans, the native tribes of North America have preserved much of their music and dance. They still perform ancient ceremonial dances, including those originally intended to bring rain, or victory in battle. These are accompanied by chanting and drums.

△ A demon spirit painted on a drumhead made of buffalo hide. The drum belonged to one of the tribes from the Great Plains in North America and was beaten to ward off evil spirits. Rattles, too, were used for this purpose.

▽ This Inuit Nootka rattle is shaped like a killer whale. The Nootkas live in and around Vancouver, Canada, and once hunted whales in dugout canoes.

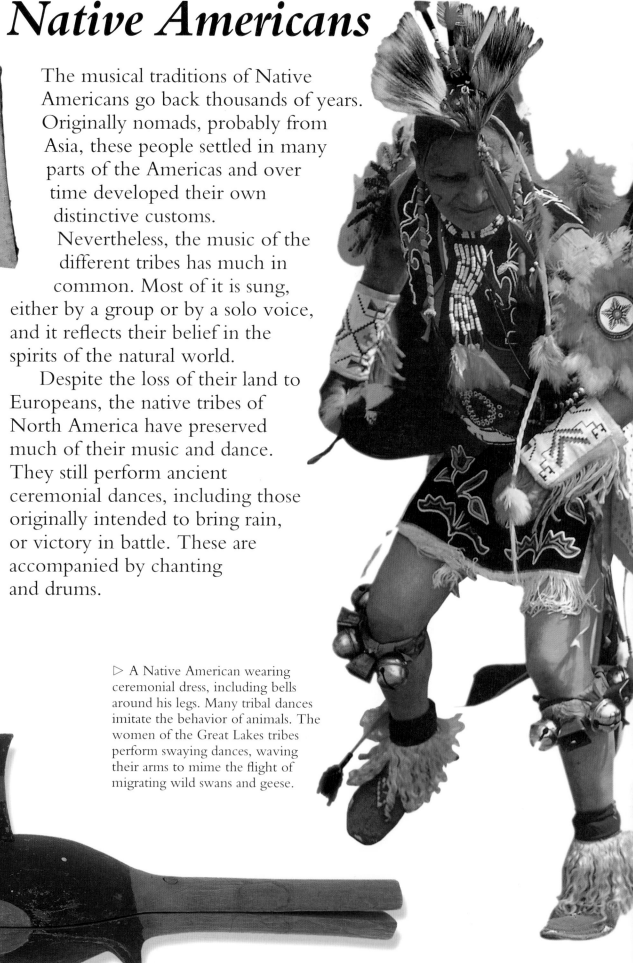

▷ A Native American wearing ceremonial dress, including bells around his legs. Many tribal dances imitate the behavior of animals. The women of the Great Lakes tribes perform swaying dances, waving their arms to mime the flight of migrating wild swans and geese.

▷ These Native
Americans are participating
in a gathering of tribes to
celebrate their musical culture.
This one takes place each year
in Gallup, New Mexico.

▷ Inuit musicians beat
vigorously on frame drums
as they sing. They also make
"mouth music," adding
grunts, hisses, snorts, and
whistles as they sing.

TIME LINE

♀ **c. 35,000 B.C.**
Native Americans first
arrive from Asia

☞ **c. A.D. 700**
Mogollon, Anasazi,
and Hoho Kam
cultures flourishing in
south-western North
America

☞ **1830s** Many
Native Americans are
forced by the U.S.
government to leave
their lands and move
west onto reservations

☞ **1861–1865**
Civil War

♀ **1869** First trans-
continental railroad
completed

☞ **1876** Sioux Chief
Sitting Bull defeats and
kills General Custer
at Battle of Little
Big Horn

☞ **1886** Apache Chief
Geronimo surrenders
to U.S. Army

▽ The Native tribes
of North America
are thought to have
migrated from northern
Asia over 35,000 years
ago when a land bridge
still existed between
Alaska and Siberia.

European Folk Music

Europe has a rich tradition of folk music. This is music that is a part of everyday life and is made by ordinary people. It is often accompanied by song and is passed down the generations by being listened to, rather than by being written down.

Every region in Europe—from the harsher northern lands to the sunnier southern countries—has its own folk music. Some instruments are typical of certain countries. The lute, for example, is common in Greece.

It is hard to estimate the age of much folk music—one of its characteristics is that tunes and words may be reshaped with each performance, hiding the music's origin. Many of the folk songs we know today date back at least as far as the Middle Ages. Troubadours wandered all over Europe, picking up tales and legends, mixing folk ideas with courtly themes. Some folk songs deal with love, some are work songs, others celebrate the change in the seasons or important events. Many are for children. The music is often danced by groups in patterns of chains, lines, and circles.

△ The Greek god Apollo plays his lyre. In ancient times, poet-musicians such as Homer sang of epic battles and heroic deeds. Their words and melodies have been remembered and passed on in the folk music of various European countries.

▽ Ukrainian Cossack dancers are well known for their high leaps and kicks. Cossacks were originally peasant soldiers who fought for the Russian army.

△ The hurdy-gurdy dates from the 1100s. Musicians around that time sang at dances or rich people's feasts, accompanying themselves with instruments such as the rebec and the hurdy-gurdy.

△ English Morris dancers wear bells on their legs to beat out the rhythms and are usually accompanied by an accordion. The Morris dance was originally a fertility ritual to encourage spring rains to fall on crops.

▷ A French street organist plays a beautifully crafted harmonium for passers-by. A bellows causes air to vibrate along the reed pipes of this keyboard instrument.

TIME LINE

☞ **c. 490 B.C.** Birth of Pericles and golden age of Greece

☞ **58–50 B.C.** Julius Caesar conquers Gaul and lands in Britain

☞ **A.D. 800** Charlemagne crowned emperor of the Holy Roman Empire

☞ **1346** Black Death enters Europe

☞ **1381** Peasants' Revolt in England

🎭 **1812** Grimm Brothers' collection of German folk tales published

♪ **1902** Composer Vaughan Williams begins collection of English folk songs

♪ **1905** Composer Béla Bartók begins collection of Hungarian folk songs

☞ **1939–1945** World War II

☞ **1957** Treaty of Rome, founding the European Community

▽ Europe stretches from the Ural Mountains to the Atlantic Ocean, and from the North Cape in Norway to the southern tip of Spain.

The Middle Ages

The Middle Ages span almost a thousand years of European history. They began with the breakup of the western Roman Empire in the A.D. 470s, and ended in the 1400s, when some of the countries we know today were beginning to take shape. In the early Middle Ages, the Christian Church began to develop a type of music known as Gregorian chant, or plainsong. Based on early Jewish religious music, plainsong was sung, or chanted, in unison and without any accompanying instruments.

In around A.D. 1000, Guido d'Arezzo, a Benedictine monk, invented staff notation. This way of writing down music in parts had a major impact on the way music was sung. Western music moved away from its Middle Eastern origins and developed harmony, which is writing two or more notes to be played together in the form of chords. In the mid-1300s, Guillaume de Machaut was celebrated for the harmonies and beauty of his music. For the first time, composers were recognized as artists with their own individual styles.

△ In this illuminated manuscript from the 1070s, King David plucks a harp. Below him a minstrel plays a rebec, an early ancestor of the violin.

△ Guido d'Arezzo, shown here on the left, invented staff notation. This way of writing down notes is still used today.

▽ "Summer is Coming in," an English song composed around 1310, celebrates the end of winter. The words are written in Middle English and Latin.

WANDERING MUSICIANS

Outside the Church, a whole range of secular (nonreligious) music was performed during the Middle Ages. From about A.D. 1000, students known as Goliards began to wander from court to court across Europe reciting poetry and songs. Jongleurs were traveling performers who entertained audiences in towns and villages with music, juggling, and acrobatic feats. During the late 1100s and 1200s, poet-musicians called troubadours sang tales of courtly love and chivalry. Many troubadours were knights and noblemen.

◁ In the Middle Ages, Christians believed that the end of the world would be heralded by angels blowing trumpets. This picture was painted in Germany during the 1400s.

TIME LINE

☞ **A.D. 476** End of the Roman Empire in Europe

♪ **590–600** Gregory I makes collection of plainsong

🎭 **698** Lindisfarne Gospel, was produced in England

♪ **750s** Wind organs first developed

☞ **800** Charlemagne becomes first Holy Roman Emperor

🎭 **800s** Romanesque style of architecture emerges in Europe

♪ **c. 1000** Guido d'Arezzo invents staff notation

☞ **1066** William of Normandy becomes King of England

♪ **1120s** Rise of troubadours in France

♪ **1150** Notre Dame School of Music is founded

🎭 **1230** Gothic cathedral of Chartres, France, is completed

♪ **c. 1250** Motet form of singing develops

♀ **1276** First paper mill built, in Italy

♪ **1350** Clavichord, an early keyboard instrument, invented

🎭 **1386–1400** Chaucer's *Canterbury Tales* written

The Renaissance

Meaning literally "rebirth," the Renaissance was a time when art and learning were revived. It began in Italy in the late 1300s and, over the next two centuries, spread throughout Europe. Also at this time, people began exploring the rest of the world and challenging accepted beliefs.

The music of the Renaissance had a new depth and richness. It often consisted of several melodic lines, or tunes, played or sung at the same time. This is called polyphony. Some splendid choral polyphonic music was written by composers from northern France and Flanders, such as Guillaume Dufay and Josquin Desprez.

Religious music was deeply affected by the Protestant Reformation of the 1500s. Wishing to give the people a more active part in worship, the reformers provided simple hymns for them to sing. In response, the Roman Catholic Church provided new and easier-to-follow music for its worshipers.

Many developments took place in nonreligious music. Gentlefolk enjoyed courtly dancing, as well as playing and singing music for their own entertainment. A favorite form of song was the madrigal, which was arranged to be sung by several people. These songs, usually about love, capture the self-confidence of this new age.

△ In this title page illustration from a book of his Masses, the Italian composer, Palestrina, presents his works to Pope Julius III.

◁ The *lira da braccio*, an early relative of the violin, had five strings that were bowed, plus two that vibrated. It was often used to accompany poetry about fictitious heroes and gods.

▽ Thomas Tallis was one of the best-known composers in the reign of Queen Elizabeth I. He wrote numerous works for the English Church, including a choral work with 40 separate parts, *Spem in alium.*

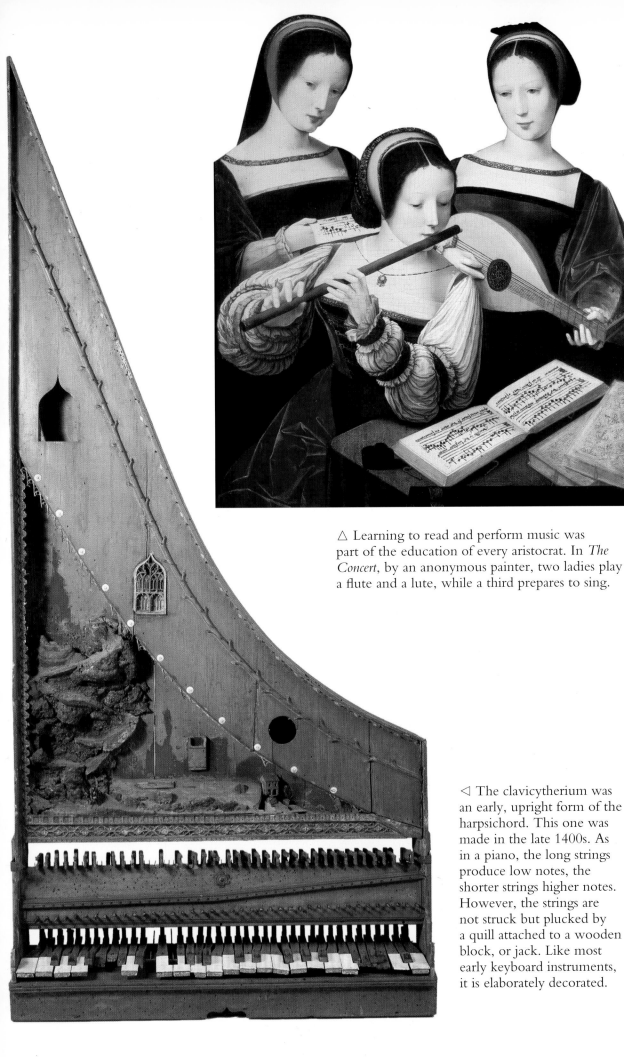

△ Learning to read and perform music was part of the education of every aristocrat. In *The Concert*, by an anonymous painter, two ladies play a flute and a lute, while a third prepares to sing.

◁ The clavicytherium was an early, upright form of the harpsichord. This one was made in the late 1400s. As in a piano, the long strings produce low notes, the shorter strings higher notes. However, the strings are not struck but plucked by a quill attached to a wooden block, or jack. Like most early keyboard instruments, it is elaborately decorated.

The Baroque Period

During the Baroque period (about 1600 to 1750), music became increasingly complex. Both instrumental and vocal music contained passages of many quick notes in rapid succession, which required great skill to perform. Singers were expected to give excitement to slower melodies by adding their own notes.

Music became more dramatic, featuring contrasts between loud and soft, fast and slow, large groups of performers and small ones. Drama and passion found their perfect outlet in a brand-new musical form called opera. This developed from spectacular court entertainments in Italy in the early 1600s. Soon public opera houses were springing up all over Europe and leading opera singers became well-known celebrities.

One of the leading Baroque composers, Johann Sebastian Bach, wrote music for the harpsichord and organ. His fugues—complicated pieces of music—evoke images of moving, three-dimensional puzzles.

△ Claudio Monteverdi was the first great composer of opera. He wrote religious music for groups of performers placed up in the church galleries to create a kind of heavenly dialogue.

▷ The Crook horn was an 18th-century version of the basic horn. By attaching different crooks (coiled tubes), the player could produce tones in different keys.

◁ The ceiling and interior of this Baroque church, with its swirling plasterwork and frolicking cherubs, fits in perfectly with the music of the period. Both are lavishly decorated and extravagant, and both appeal to the emotions.

◁ Johann Sebastian Bach is shown here at the keyboard, surrounded by some of his many children and his second wife, Anna Magdalena *(standing center)*. Several of Bach's sons became important composers.

▽ George Frideric Handel was best known as a composer of operas and oratorios. His most famous oratorio is *Messiah*. Handel also produced a great deal of music for the orchestra, including the *Water Music*.

TIME LINE

♪ **1607** First performance of Monteverdi's opera *Orfeo* in Mantua, Italy

⚔ **1642–1648** English Civil War

💡 **1687** Sir Isaac Newton's theory of gravity published

♪ **c. 1700** The piano is invented

⚒ **1703** Czar Peter the Great of Russia begins building St. Petersburg

🎭 **1719** Ancient city of Pompeii discovered in Italy

♪ **1729** First performance of Bach's *St Matthew Passion*

♪ **1742** First performance of Handel's *Messiah* in Dublin

🎭 **1755** Samuel Johnson's dictionary of the English language published

The Classical Age

△ This plaque made in the late 1700s shows Homer playing the lyre. In this period, Greek art was much admired. Classical composers aimed for an equally harmonious effect in their music.

▽ Music was a vital part of court life, especially at the court of Frederick the Great of Prussia. As well as composing music, he was an accomplished player of the flute.

Around the mid–1700s, the Baroque style began to seem old-fashioned. People now preferred music that was more restrained and balanced. These qualities were characteristic of the art of ancient Greece and Rome, the "classical" civilizations, and gave this period which lasted into the 1820s, its name. However, some of the musical forms from the Baroque period remained popular, evolving to suit the new taste and improved instruments. Among them was the solo concerto, a piece of music written for an orchestra but featuring a specific instrument. Mozart wrote 21 piano concertos.

New forms, too, were created. The symphony, a work for the orchestra, usually in four contrasting movements, was developed, and perfected by Franz Joseph Haydn. Like the concerto, it attracted large audiences to public concerts, now an important part of the musical scene. The string quartet and other pieces written for small groups also became very popular.

◁ Franz Joseph Haydn's opera *L'incontro Improvviso* (The Unexpected Encounter) was first performed at the palace of the Esterházy family in Hungary. The conductor, seated at the keyboard as was the custom, may be Haydn himself.

▷ Wolfgang Amadeus Mozart (*center*) was a brilliant keyboard player as well as a composer. Here, he is seen with his sister and his father, Leopold.

◁ In this scene from the 1818 Munich production of Mozart's opera *The Magic Flute*, designed by Simon Quaglio, the Queen of the Night makes a dramatic entrance. This opera contains some of the loveliest music Mozart ever wrote—produced at a time (1791) when he was racked with debt and illness.

Beethoven

▽ A death mask of Beethoven. Such masks, modeled directly on the dead person's face, were used to commemorate famous people.

The world into which Ludwig van Beethoven was born, in 1770, was on the brink of great changes. When he was five years old, the American Colonies declared their independence from Britain; when he was 22, the French king was guillotined by revolutionaries. There was a new interest in heroic figures as reflected in the poems of Byron. It is not surprising that *Fidelio,* the one opera Beethoven wrote, is about heroism and the fight for freedom.

▷ *Napoleon Crossing the Alps,* by Jacques-Louis David, shows the general in heroic form, intent on conquest. Napoleon Bonaparte came to power in France as a leader of the revolution against foreign enemies, then went on to bring other parts of Europe under French rule.

▷ Beethoven originally dedicated his third symphony, the *Eroica,* to Napoleon Bonaparte, whom he greatly admired. But when he learned that his hero had made himself emperor, Beethoven scratched out the original dedication and wrote "Heroic Symphony, composed to celebrate the memory of a great man."

In Beethoven's music we find a change taking place from the elegant style typical of the 1700s to the more dramatic, personal approach that would dominate the 1800s. Some of his early piano sonatas, contain music of great tenderness. But there are also turbulent passages, such as the first movement of the *Pathétique* sonata (1799), a hint of his later works, in which he developed ideas in greater depth, producing very intense and fiery music.

▽ This portrait of Beethoven, at work on his *Missa Solemnis* (Solemn Mass), was painted by Joseph Carl Steiler when the composer was 49. It shows him as handsome and soulful. He died in 1827, at age 56.

△ Some of the ear trumpets that Beethoven used after he realized, in the late 1790s, that he was going deaf. Although he could still hear music in his head well enough to compose, he could no longer play or conduct.

The Romantic Spirit

△ These musical kittens, scrambling over the staves, are generally believed to have been drawn by Schubert. But the artist was probably one of the composer's friends, Moritz von Schwind.

In the early 1800s, the arts focused on themes that we call "romantic." These included the beauty of nature, the power of the imagination, and the supernatural. There was also a new interest in the art and music of the Middle Ages. These themes were explored by composers such as Franz Liszt and Hector Berlioz.

Liszt invented a new single-movement musical form, called the symphonic poem, to convey his personal interpretation of dramatic themes or stories. Franz Schubert wrote hundreds of songs both as settings for Romantic poems and to express his feelings of longing and sadness. Other composers used the symphony to evoke dreams and emotions. Berlioz's *Symphonie Fantastique,* for example, describes in part "fantastic" scenes from his own vivid imagination.

△ The dazzling technique of the violinist Nicolò Paganini (1782–1840), and his strange, dark features, led to claims that he was possessed by the devil.

◁ Unlike classical concertos, in which solo and orchestra were well-balanced, those by Franz Liszt were mainly a showcase for the soloist. This cartoon shows Liszt, with keyboard wings, delivering a mortal blow to the orchestra's "General Bass."

▷ The upper scenes of *The Symphony*, by Moritz von Schwind, suggest different themes for a composition. In the bottom scene the finished work is being performed. Franz Schubert can be seen standing in the background, third from left.

◁ Frédéric Chopin (seen here in a photograph taken in the 1840s) was one of the greatest pianists of the age, although he only performed in public 30 times. Most of his compositions are for piano, and many are based on the folk dances of his native Poland.

TIME LINE

♪ **1813** Franz Schubert writes his *Symphony no. 1*

♪ **1824** First performance of Beethoven's *Symphony no. 9*

☞ **1832** Greece achieves independence from Ottoman Empire

✾ **1838** J. M. W. Turner paints *The Fighting Téméraire*

♪ **1846** First performance of Felix Mendelssohn's oratorio *Elijah*, in England.

♀ **1851** The Great Exhibition held in London

☞ **1854–1856** The Crimean War

✾ **1857** Publication of Gustave Flaubert's novel *Madame Bovary*

Late Romanticism

In the late 1800s, symphonies became longer and required even larger orchestras. Gustav Mahler's *Symphony no. 3* requires a huge orchestra, two choirs, and a solo singer. It has six movements and lasts about 90 minutes. Music also continued to be used as a way of expressing emotion. A powerful example is Pyotr Ilyich Tchaikovsky's last symphony, *Symphony no. 6*, which has been called a "symphonic suicide note."

The work of other composers, such as Modest Mussorgsky, Nicolai Rimsky-Korsakov, Antonin Dvořák, and Edvard Grieg illustrate a new trend—nationalism. This kind of music often included folk elements to help express patriotism. The operas of Richard Wagner drew their stories mainly from Germanic legend, but the music was startlingly original. Traditionally, opera had comprised songs (arias and choruses), linked by recitative (a kind of sung speech). Richard Wagner replaced this structure with a continuous flow of music containing short melodic pieces called *leitmotifs*. Each *leitmotif* represented a character, place, object, idea, or feeling. Giuseppe Verdi's operas contained more traditional harmonies. His glorious melodies, driving rhythms, and dramatic stories brought Italian opera to a new peak.

△ Richard Wagner's *Ring*, a cycle made up of four operas, was his crowning achievement. Over some 18 hours (with intermissions), it tells a story of love, heroism, greed, and treachery. This is a scene from the last opera, *The Twilight of the Gods.*

▽ Johannes Brahms' music combines romanticism with a preference for classical structure. He also loved folk music. Shown here is one of his *Hungarian Dances.*

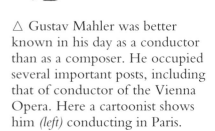

△ Gustav Mahler was better known in his day as a conductor than as a composer. He occupied several important posts, including that of conductor of the Vienna Opera. Here a cartoonist shows him (*left*) conducting in Paris.

△ The lighter side of Viennese music was captured in the dances of Johann Strauss the Younger. This cartoon, drawn after his death, shows him in heaven conducting one of his waltzes. Around him dance the ghosts of other composers, including his friend Brahms *(third from right)*, Bach, Mozart, and Beethoven.

▷ A scene from Giuseppe Verdi's *Nabucco* (Nebuchadnezzar), which is about the Hebrews' captivity in Babylon. Verdi's patriotism—he was a fervent supporter of the unification of Italy—can be heard in this opera's stirring choruses, as well as in some of his other operas.

TIME LINE

⚔ **1861–1865** Civil War

🎭 **1869** Leo Tolstoy's novel *War and Peace* published

⚔ **1870** Unification of Italy completed

🎭 **1869** First exhibition of Impressionist painting, in Paris

♪ **1871** First performance of Verdi's opera *Aida*

♪ **1871** First performance of Wagner's *Ring,* in Bayreuth, Germany

💡 **1877** Thomas Edison invents the phonograph (wax cylinder-type model)

⚔ **1883** Eruption of Mount Krakatoa, in Indonesia, killing 36,000 people

💡 **1895** X rays discovered by Wilhelm Röntgen

♪ **1899** First performance of Sir Edward Elgar's "Enigma" Variations, in Birmingham, England

Music of the Modern Age

The music of our own century has undergone many changes. In the early 1900s, Debussy was using sounds to suggest images in a similar way to Impressionist painting. Although his harmonies were new, they presented no great challenge to audiences. The real shock came with Igor Stravinsky's ballet *The Rite of Spring*. With its violent, hammering rhythms, it caused a riot at its Paris première.

At the same time, Arnold Schoenberg was developing his 12-tone system, in which the sense of key was eliminated. Other composers later adopted this system, including Karlheinz Stockhausen.

A later development was random music, in which the sounds produced are decided either by the performers (who are given only guidelines) or by chance. The main figure in this movement was John Cage. He used all sorts of sounds, from radio static to fragments of speech, in his pieces.

Minimalism, which emerged in the early 1960s, is the repetition or gradual variation of a short theme over a long period. Leading minimalist composers include Philip Glass, Steve Reich, and Arvo Pärt.

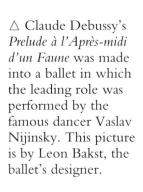

△ Claude Debussy's *Prelude à l'Après-midi d'un Faune* was made into a ballet in which the leading role was performed by the famous dancer Vaslav Nijinsky. This picture is by Leon Bakst, the ballet's designer.

▷ Igor Stravinsky, shown here at work, is arguably the most important composer of the 1900s. For nearly 60 years he drew on influences, and music ranging from classical to jazz.

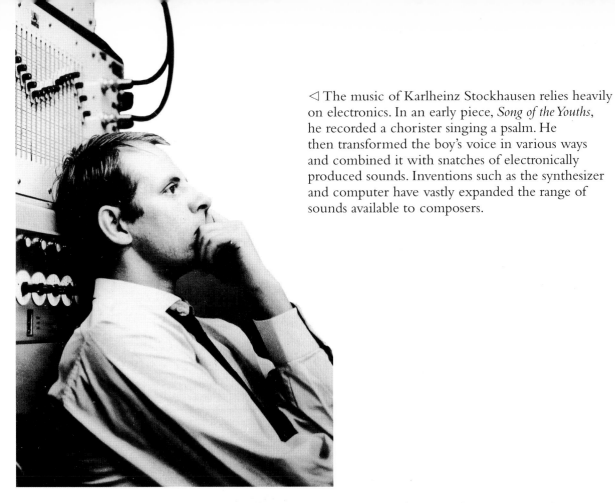

◁ The music of Karlheinz Stockhausen relies heavily on electronics. In an early piece, *Song of the Youths,* he recorded a chorister singing a psalm. He then transformed the boy's voice in various ways and combined it with snatches of electronically produced sounds. Inventions such as the synthesizer and computer have vastly expanded the range of sounds available to composers.

▷ *The Cave,* by minimalist composer Steve Reich, is a multimedia work based on the biblical figure, Abraham. As well as a traditional chamber orchestra and four singers, the piece makes use of the latest video technology. The words and pictures that accompany the music are projected onto five large screens.

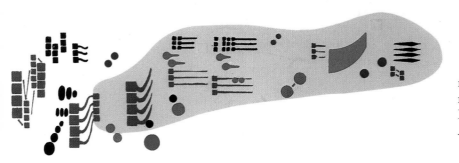

◁ The sounds for some modern music require completely new kinds of notation. These colored marks are for Györgi Ligeti's electronic piece *Artikulations.*

Jazz

Jazz was born in the 1890s in the southern city of New Orleans. African-Americans combined the energy and rhythms of African music with the sounds and instruments of the Western world. It was the beginning of a totally new style of music. Condemned at first as "the Devil's music," jazz nevertheless soon spread across the United States and later the world. Its power to dazzle audiences has long been associated with brilliant instrumentalists such as the brass player Louis Armstrong and the pianist Duke Ellington. Along with the famous players, singers such as Bessie Smith and Billie Holiday also emerged as important musicians.

In the 1930s, dance band leaders Benny Goodman and Glenn Miller brought a new style of jazz called "swing" to a much wider audience. After World War II, increasingly complex music was developed by pioneers like Charlie Parker and Miles Davis. Today, all jazz styles—from traditional New Orleans to the recent fusion between jazz and rock—remain popular.

△ Top New Orleans jazzman Joe "King" Oliver moved north to Chicago in 1920. With rising star Louis Armstrong playing cornet alongside him, Oliver's classic 1923 recordings helped the spread of jazz throughout the United States.

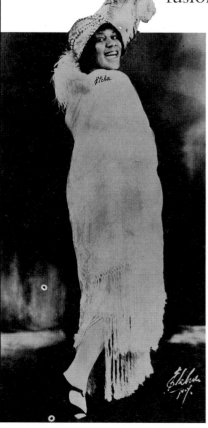

▷ Bessie Smith was one of the earliest jazz singers. Known as the "Empress of the Blues," she sang in the blues scale. Unique to jazz and blues, this scale has a mournful and expressive sound.

△ In the late 1930s, trombonist Glenn Miller led the top "swing" band in the United States. Hits such as "In the Mood" brought jazz to a wider and younger audience. Miller's performances ended in 1944 when, on a flight to Paris during World War II, his airplane disappeared over the English Channel without trace.

▷ An inspiring pianist, Thelonious Monk helped Charlie Parker and others create "bebop." Often fast and furious, the new jazz shocked more traditional fans. Monk's "Round Midnight" is one of the most recorded jazz tunes of all time.

◁ The blistering cornet solos of Louis "Satchmo" Armstrong took the jazz world by storm in the 1920s. Armstrong's mastery over the trumpet was equally superb, and singing in his distinctive growl, he went on to become a worldwide star.

▷ The brilliant technique of Wynton Marsalis has made him one of the most acclaimed jazz musicians playing today. He is equally at home playing classical music for trumpet.

TIME LINE

☞ **1863** Slavery abolished in the United States

♪ **1890s** Development of ragtime

♪ **1903** Bessie Smith makes singing debut aged 9

☞ **1914** Outbreak of World War I

♪ **1920s** King Oliver and Jelly Roll Morton develop New Orleans jazz in Chicago and New York

🎭 **1927** *The Jazz Singer* released in U.S. movie theaters.

☞ **1939** Outbreak of World War II

♪ **1940s** Start of the "bebop" revolution

♪ **1955** Miles Davis stars at Newport Jazz Festival

♪ **1960s** Development of avant garde "free" jazz

☞ **1963** Assassination of President John F. Kennedy

♪ **1970s** Early jazz-rock fusion experiments

♪ **1991** Death of Miles Davis

Musicals

The musical is a marriage of operetta, or light opera, and the British and American music hall acts of the 1890s. The composer Irving Berlin added one other vital ingredient—jazz. Early musicals had very thin story lines and the songs were little more than decoration. This all changed in the late 1920s with Jerome Kern's groundbreaking shows, especially *Show Boat*, which made the songs central to the story and covered more serious subjects.

In the 1930s the sophisticated music and lyrics of Cole Porter, George and Ira Gershwin, Richard Rodgers, and Lorenz Hart became popular. But it was Rodgers and Hammerstein's *Oklahoma!* that, in 1943, ushered in the golden age of the Broadway musical. Stephen Sondheim, a pupil of Hammerstein's, emerged as a brilliant composer in the late 1950s. More recently rock music has made its influence felt, and in the 1970s and 1980s British shows, especially those of Andrew Lloyd Webber, began to dominate the world of musicals.

△ Irving Berlin made jazz an important part of musicals. He wrote the music and lyrics for a string of hits—even though he never learned how to read or write music.

▽ *Show Boat*, first performed in 1927, was Jerome Kern's masterpiece. It was one of the first musicals in which the songs, such as "Ol' Man River," are central to the story.

▷ *Oklahoma!* opened in 1943, beginning 30 years of worldwide dominance for the Broadway musical. It boasted a ballet, superb songs, and a dramatic story line. It was songwriter Oscar Hammerstein II's and composer Richard Rodgers' first show together.

◁ *Singin' in the Rain*, which appeared in 1952, is considered one of the greatest screen musicals. The movie, starring Gene Kelly, makes fun of the "talkies" (movies with recorded sound).

△ For over 70 years New York's Broadway has been the home of American musicals. Today, shows from Britain, such as *Les Misérables*, also enjoy great critical and public acclaim.

△ Packed with romance and mystery, *The Phantom of the Opera* is one of Andrew Lloyd Webber's most spectacular shows. Other smash hits include *Starlight Express* and *Cats*.

West Side Story

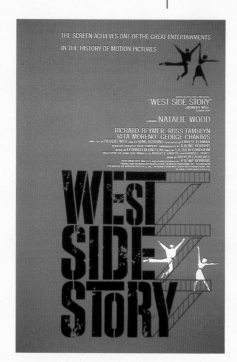

THE SCREEN ACHIEVES ONE OF THE GREAT ENTERTAINMENTS
IN THE HISTORY OF MOTION PICTURES

"WEST SIDE STORY"

NATALIE WOOD

RICHARD BEYMER · RUSS TAMBLYN
RITA MORENO · GEORGE CHAKIRIS

WEST SIDE STORY

△ Great musicals do not always make great films. *West Side Story* is one that did. The 1961 movie was a worldwide hit.

△ Leonard Bernstein (*right*) already had a successful career as a conductor and composer behind him when he teamed up with newcomer Stephen Sondheim (*left*) to write the music for *West Side Story*.

In 1957, *West Side Story* brought musical theater up to date with a bang. The show took Shakespeare's classic love story *Romeo and Juliet* and moved it to the violent streets of New York City. Director and choreographer Jerome Robbins came up with the original concept, but like all great musicals, the end product was the result of successful teamwork. The combined talents of writer Arthur Laurents, composer Leonard Bernstein, lyricist Stephen Sondheim, and Robbins himself proved to be a winning formula.

Four years after its Broadway opening, *West Side Story* was made into a dazzling movie that went on to win two Academy Awards. With its depiction of prejudice, passion, and gang warfare, both the screen version and stage show remain as powerful as ever for today's audiences.

ROMEO AND JULIET

First performed in 1596, *Romeo and Juliet* has always been one of Shakespeare's most popular plays. It tells the story of two young lovers from Verona, Italy, caught up in a bitter feud between their families, the Montagues and the Capulets. After Romeo and Juliet are secretly married, Romeo is exiled from Verona for killing a Capulet. The play ends with the two lovers taking their own lives. As well as *West Side Story*, this tragic story has inspired six operas, Tchaikovsky's *Romeo and Juliet Fantasy Overture*, and a ballet by Prokofiev. There have also been many movies of the play, including seven silent versions as well as Franco Zeffirelli's famous 1968 movie.

The writer Arthur Laurents turned Shakespeare's feuding Montagues and Capulets into rival gangs, the Jets and the Sharks. Ex-Jet Tony falls in love with Maria, sister of the Sharks' leader Bernardo. In a gang fight Bernardo kills Riff, the Jets' leader, with a knife. Tony then stabs Bernardo to death. *West Side Story* ends tragically, as Tony himself dies of gunshot wounds in Maria's arms.

▽ Jerome Robbins mixed ballet, jive, and Latin American dance to create the thrilling movement that fills *West Side Story*. With Robert Wise he also codirected the 1961 movie version.

▽ To create real tension between the gangs, director Jerome Robbins encouraged the actors to stay in character both on and off stage.

MOVIE CREDITS

Released—1961

Screenplay—Arthur Laurents/Ernest Lehman

Lyrics—Stephen Sondheim

Music—Leonard Bernstein

Codirector/ Choreographer— Jerome Robbins

Codirector/Producer— Robert Wise

Cast
Maria—Natalie Wood

Tony—Richard Beymer

Anita—Rita Moreno

Riff—Russ Tamblyn

Bernardo—George Chakiris

Rock and Pop

▽ Elvis Presley burst onto the U.S. pop scene in the 1950s. Singing raw rock 'n' roll and swiveling his hips, he delighted his young fans.

The term "popular music" can apply to anything from music hall ballads to salsa. "Pop" is a little more specific and includes everything from 1950s rock 'n' roll to 1990s rap. Rock 'n' roll was the first music to speak directly to young people. It mixed African-American rhythm and blues with white American country music. Elvis Presley made rock 'n' roll a worldwide phenomenon. In Britain, the Beatles added their top-selling songwriting skills to rock 'n' roll, while the Rolling Stones imitated the blues of Chicago. The Stones' loud, tough sound paved the way for the aggressive style of heavy metal.

Meanwhile, Artists such as Aretha Franklin created a new blend of rhythm and blues and gospel music, which came to be known as "soul." Disco music, which made heavy use of synthesizers, and rap music are direct descendants of soul. In the late 1970s, a new generation produced its own wild version of rock 'n' roll called punk rock. The 1980s and 1990s saw superstars, like Michael Jackson and Madonna, and groups such as U2, filling huge stadiums.

▽ In 1964, the Beatles returned home to a hero's welcome. Their first tour of the United States launched an "invasion" of British groups that inspired American bands.

▷ Johnny Rotten and his punk band, the Sex Pistols, played rock 'n' roll at a frenzied speed using crude lyrics and rude gestures.

△ Tina Turner's career spans several decades of pop music. She had her first hits in the 1960s with her then husband, Ike Turner. Her solo career took off in the 1980s with the million-selling album *Private Dancer*.

▷ Since the late 1970s, Bruce Springsteen has been one of the leading singer-guitarists, following the tradition of Eric Clapton. A sensational live performer, Springsteen also developed great skill as a songwriter.

Introduction—Part One

There are thousands of different types of instruments around the world. The variety of forms, of the simple flute, for example, is almost endless. There are also many different methods of producing sound from instruments, and this is one way of classifying them. The ancient Greeks divided their instruments into two groups, those that were blown and those that were struck.

Today, one well-known classification is that of the Western orchestra, in which instruments are arranged into families of strings, woodwind, brass, and percussion. Within these families instruments are further subdivided by the way they are played. Another popular system also divides instruments up according to the way they produce sound. This system classifies instruments into five broad groups—idiophones, membranophones, chordophones, aerophones, and electrophones.

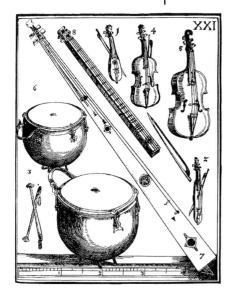

△ Members of the chordophone, or string, family shown in a book published in 1618.

IDIOPHONES AND MEMBRANOPHONES

Examples of idiophones include the triangle, castanet, cymbal, woodblock, and the xylophone. In all these instruments sound is produced by the material from which the instrument itself is made. A membranophone produces sound by making a stretched skin vibrate. Most drums are membranophones. The common name for idiophones and membranophones is percussion instruments. Together these two groups make up the first section of this chapter.

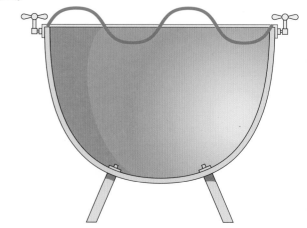

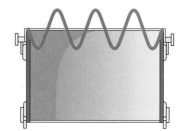

The stretched skin of a drum vibrates when it is hit. The pitch of a drumhead can be altered by tightening or loosening the vibrating skin. If the skin is made less tight then the pitch of the note it makes will be lower. If the skin is tightened, the pitch of the note played will be higher. The smaller the drum the higher the sound will be because the area of the vibrating skin is reduced.

CHORDOPHONES

In all chordophones, sound is produced by a string or strings stretched between two fixed points. Some of the most well-known examples are the violin, cello, harp, and guitar. The pitch of a string depends upon its length, thickness, and how tightly it is stretched. A short string will sound a higher pitch than a longer string. A thin string will sound a higher pitch than a thicker string. A tight string will sound a higher pitch than a looser string. Traditionally, strings were made from animal gut, hair, metal, and, in Asia, silk. Today, they are usually made from nylon, which lasts longer and is less easy to break. Chordophones are more often known as stringed instruments. This group makes up the second section of this chapter.

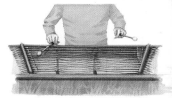

◁ On instruments such as the violin, or guitar, players sound different pitches on the same string by 'stopping' the string. Pressing the string against the fingerboard alters the vibrating length of the string and changes the pitch.

△ The violin is played with a bow made of horsehair. This is covered with rosin to make the bow "grip" the strings.

△ Plucking strings with fingers or a piece of hard material called a plectrum, produces different sounds.

△ Dulcimers are played with two wooden beaters or padded sticks that are held by the musician. Beaters can be straight or curved.

△ The sound of a vibrating string will be weak unless the string is attached to a resonator. This makes the vibrations louder. The violin's resonator is the hollow body, called a soundbox.

BANGING AND CRASHING

Some drums are played with the hands. All parts of the hands can be used, including the fingers, the knuckles, and the palm, to produce a range of different sounds.

The crash of the cymbals is one of the most exciting of all instrumental sounds. The player stops the vibrations of the cymbals by pressing them against his or her body.

Some drums are played with beaters. These can range from a pair of hard wooden sticks to sticks with a pad of soft felt at the tip. A blow with a hard stick produces a more explosive sound than a blow with a padded stick. Drums can also be played with brushes, which produce a softer sound.

Introduction—Part Two

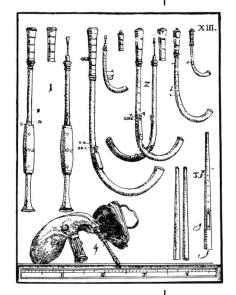

△ A drawing of early wind instruments, or aerophones, made in the early 1600s.

AEROPHONES

Wind instruments of all kinds are classed as aerophones. These are tubelike instruments that produce sound when the air blown into them vibrates. Two major groups of instruments are aerophones—woodwind (including flute, clarinet, and oboe) and brass (including trumpet, trombone, and French horn). Woodwinds have holes in them, which may be covered by "keys." Most brass instruments have valves on them (*right*). Both affect the pitch of sound produced. When a hole is stopped on a flute, or a valve pressed down on a trumpet, the air inside the instrument is "lengthened." This produces a low note.

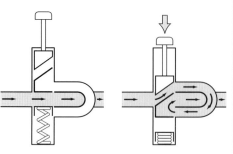

△ Pressed down, the piston valve forces air through extra tubing—the note is deepened.

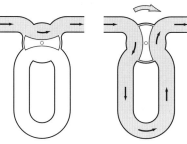

△ Rotary valves also force air through extra tubing, but are only used on French horns.

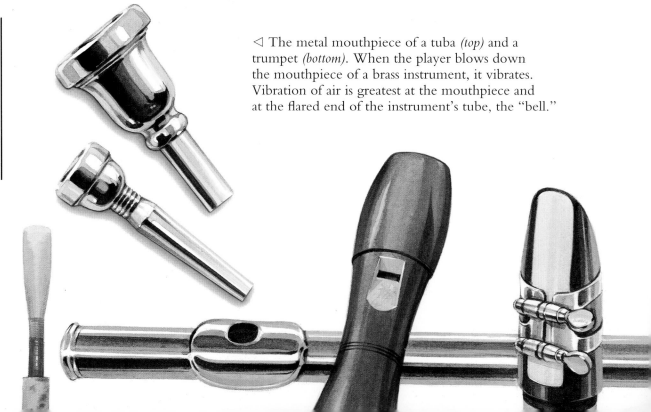

◁ The metal mouthpiece of a tuba *(top)* and a trumpet *(bottom)*. When the player blows down the mouthpiece of a brass instrument, it vibrates. Vibration of air is greatest at the mouthpiece and at the flared end of the instrument's tube, the "bell."

▷ Mouthpieces of various woodwind instruments. From left to right—oboe, flute, recorder, and clarinet. The oboe and clarinet have reeds—thin strips of cane in the mouthpiece that vibrate when blown. The recorder is a member of the flute family.

HOW KEYBOARDS WORK

The harpsichord is a plucked string instrument. When the player presses a key *(below),* a "jack" moves up and plucks the string.

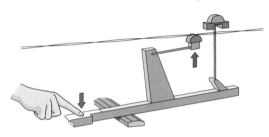

When a piano key is pressed down *(below)*, a system of levers causes a hammer to strike a tuned string. When the key is released, a "damper" stops further vibrations of the string.

ELECTROPHONES

Electrophones are musical instruments whose sounds are either picked up and amplified, or electronically generated such as the electric guitar and synthesizer. The synthesizer *(above)* can be played like a piano, while controls above the keyboard transform the notes into original and often strange sounds. The synthesizer also has a huge computer memory which can play back stored sounds while the musician improvises over them. Although the electric guitar is the best-known example in which air vibrations are converted into an electric signal, this principle can also be applied to almost any acoustic instrument—the violin, the double bass, the clarinet, the flute, the saxophone— and many others.

KEYBOARD INSTRUMENTS

Keyboard instruments are difficult to classify. The organ is strictly an aerophone, and the harpsichord and piano are strictly chordophones. The link between all these instruments is that the player presses down a key to operate a mechanism that produces the sound. The keys on a piano cause small hammers to strike tuned strings. On a harpsichord, the keys control a mechanism that plucks the strings. Pressing a key on an organ opens a pipe in which a column of air vibrates. Some of the pipes can also be operated by foot pedals.

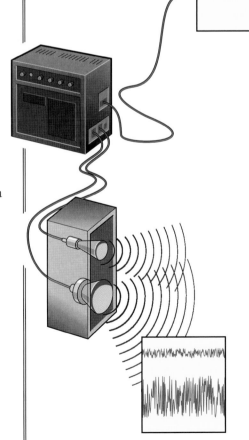

△ An electric guitar has no need of a resonator, or sound box, as an acoustic guitar does. Instead, an electronic "pickup" converts the vibrations from its strings into electric signals. These signals are passed through an amplifier, which makes them much more powerful. Loudspeakers then convert the signals into sound.

The Human Voice

The human voice is the most natural musical instrument of all. It is also one of the most expressive, whether it belongs to a folksinger or to a highly trained opera star. All singing is a complex process. Sound is produced when air from the lungs is forced past the vocal cords. Notes of different pitch are made according to how quickly or slowly these cords vibrate. Singers give expression to sound when they learn how to control their breathing and the muscles around the mouth.

All around the world people enjoy the sound of the human voice and there are endless ways of using it in a musical setting. Traditions of storytelling set to music are still very strong in China and other Far Eastern countries. In Islamic countries, the voice of a *muezzin*, or crier, summons people to prayer several times every day. And in Australia, singing forms a vital part of the Aborigine people's culture as a means of celebrating and passing on their history and beliefs.

△ Angels are said to have the purest voices of all. This sculpture from the 1400s depicts them in mid-song.

▽ The vocal cords are tightened when someone speaks or sings. Breathing out makes the cords vibrate and produce sound.

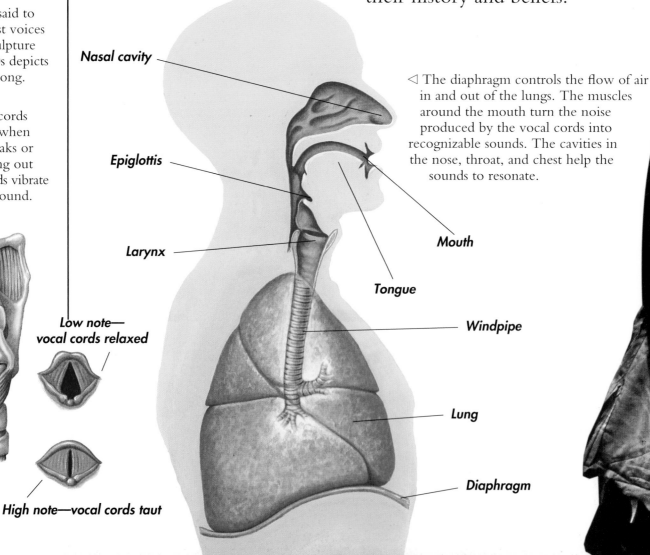

Nasal cavity

Epiglottis

Larynx

Low note— vocal cords relaxed

High note—vocal cords taut

◁ The diaphragm controls the flow of air in and out of the lungs. The muscles around the mouth turn the noise produced by the vocal cords into recognizable sounds. The cavities in the nose, throat, and chest help the sounds to resonate.

Mouth

Tongue

Windpipe

Lung

Diaphragm

VOCAL RANGE

The natural pitch range of the human voice depends upon the shape and size of the throat and mouth. Men have deeper voices than women because they generally have larger larynxes with longer vocal cords. Women's voices fall into three ranges—soprano, mezzo-soprano, and contralto (in descending order of pitch). The tenor, baritone, and bass are the male equivalents.

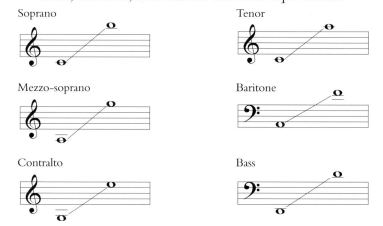

Soprano

Tenor

Mezzo-soprano

Baritone

Contralto

Bass

△ Boy sopranos, or trebles, have sung in European church and cathedral choirs since the Middle Ages. This practice dates from times when women were forbidden to sing in church. Today, however, some services are also sung by girls' choirs.

◁ In many operas, the tenor voice is used to sing the part of the hero, the soprano voice that of the heroine and the bass voice that of the villain.

△ The technique of singing into a microphone is quite different from opera singing. Opera singers have to "throw," or project, their voices so that people some distance away can hear them. Singers who use microphones have their voices projected electronically.

LISTEN FOR

BOY'S TREBLE
Geoffrey Burgon—
Nunc Dimittis

CHORAL WORKS
George Frideric Handel—
Messiah

Wolfgang Amadeus Mozart
—*Requiem*

OPERAS
Gioachino Rossini—
The Barber of Seville

Giacomo Puccini—
Madama Butterfly

WORLD MUSIC
Songs by Salif Keita, Miriam Makeba, and Youssou N'Dour

LATIN AMERICAN MUSIC
Songs by Celia Cruz, Joe Arroyo, and Joao Gilberto

Drums

From the earliest times, drums have been associated with magic and ritual, pounded in battles and parades, or used to send messages over long distances. A drumbeat provides the pulse that drives the music forward in a Native American ceremonial dance or an explosive rock 'n' roll song. In Western orchestras drums often bring a symphony to a dramatic and thunderous climax.

Many drums have a skin stretched tightly across a frame. When the skin is struck by a beater or a hand, its vibrations give out the sound. Some instruments, such as the kettledrums, or timpani, have to be carefully tuned to the correct pitch. Others, such as the Japanese *tsuzumi*, have to be struck with exactly the right force. And a good sense of rhythm is always vital.

△ In this picture, painted in the 1800s, a frame drum beats out the rhythm for this Native American buffalo dance. Most frame drums are made of thin wood and skin and are light enough to hold in one hand.

▷ A modern Western orchestra usually has two or three kettledrums, or timpani. The timpanist can change the pitch of the instrument by moving the foot pedal up and down. The pedal is attached to tension rods that tighten or loosen the drumhead.

Drumsticks have padded ends

Tension rod

Tuning gauge indicates pitch of drumhead

Foot pedal changes pitch of drum

△ The Indian *tabla* is made up of two drums, each tuned to a different pitch. The player strikes the drumheads with the fingers of both hands.

PERCUSSION

In a Western orchestra, all the percussion instruments are located at the rear. They may include timpani, a gong, a xylophone, a side drum, and a bass drum.

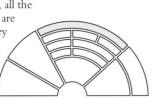

▷ The *tsuzumi*, from Japan, is a small handheld drum. A silk cord secures the skins at either end. The player can change the pitch of the drum by squeezing the cord to tighten the skin.

Drumhead made of plastic or calfskin

Connecting mechanism links tension rod with drumhead

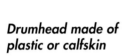

Supporting strut

Bowl made of copper

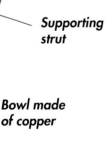

Wheel makes drum easier to move

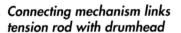

▽ The twirling drum is a small drum on a stick. When the drum is spun around, two balls rattle against the drumhead.

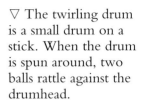

▽ British musician Evelyn Glennie (born 1965) is famous for her solo performances on a wide range of percussion instruments. She is deaf, but feels the vibrations of the music through her sense of touch.

ATTACHING THE DRUMHEAD

In some drums the stretched skin, or drumhead, is laced to a second skin at the other end of the frame.

In many drums a metal hoop, tightened around the top of the instrument, holds the drumhead in place.

Sometimes the drumhead is secured by gluing it to the frame. It can also be nailed or pegged in place.

Gongs, Rattles, and Bells

There are many percussion instruments on which it is possible to play tunes. Most of these have a set of bars of different lengths, which sound out different pitches when they are struck. The bars can be made of wood, metal, or even stone. Instruments with wooden bars are called xylophones. Metallaphones have metal bars, and lithophones have bars of stone. Other tuned percussion instruments have gongs instead of bars. Gong instruments are an important part of the *gamelan* orchestras of Java and Bali. Rattles and jingles are simple percussion instruments that come to life when they are shaken. Rattles can be fashioned from a whole range of materials including wood, clay, animal shells, and dried seed pods. Jingles are small tinkling bells that are often worn by dancers around their ankles and wrists. Much larger and louder are the struck bells that ring out from temples across the Far East.

△ Jingles attached to the ankles and arms of this Indian dancer provide a tinkling accompaniment to all her movements.

▽ The stone chime is one of the oldest Chinese instruments, dating back more than 7,000 years. The stones are cut into L-shapes of varying thickness so that each one has a different pitch. The stone chime was played at dances, banquets, and other ceremonial occasions.

Gong with lowest pitch

Seeds threaded onto net

Hollow gourd

◁ Some rattles are made from dried vegetable shells, or gourds. When this Nigerian rattle is shaken, seeds strung onto a net strike the body of the gourd.

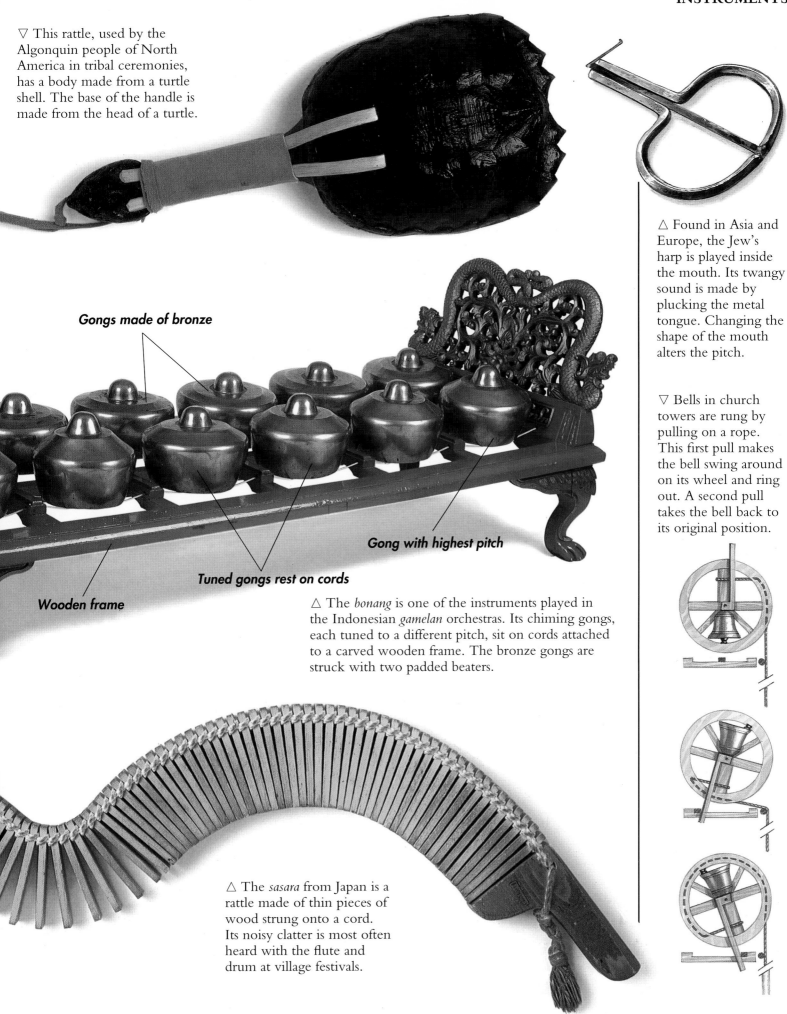

▽ This rattle, used by the Algonquin people of North America in tribal ceremonies, has a body made from a turtle shell. The base of the handle is made from the head of a turtle.

Gongs made of bronze

Gong with highest pitch

Tuned gongs rest on cords

Wooden frame

△ The *bonang* is one of the instruments played in the Indonesian *gamelan* orchestras. Its chiming gongs, each tuned to a different pitch, sit on cords attached to a carved wooden frame. The bronze gongs are struck with two padded beaters.

△ The *sasara* from Japan is a rattle made of thin pieces of wood strung onto a cord. Its noisy clatter is most often heard with the flute and drum at village festivals.

△ Found in Asia and Europe, the Jew's harp is played inside the mouth. Its twangy sound is made by plucking the metal tongue. Changing the shape of the mouth alters the pitch.

▽ Bells in church towers are rung by pulling on a rope. This first pull makes the bell swing around on its wheel and ring out. A second pull takes the bell back to its original position.

Guitars, Harps, and Lutes

The guitar is played all over the world. It can be used to accompany singing or dancing, or it can be played as a solo instrument. Probably introduced into Spain by the Arabs, it was established throughout Europe by the late 1300s. Modern guitars include the folk guitar, classical guitar, flamenco guitar, and electric guitar. But the most ancient string instrument is the musical bow, a single string tied at both ends to a flexible stick, that may be 16,000 years old. Harps and lyres also date back thousands of years—they were first played in Egypt about 5,000 years ago. The lyre survives only in parts of Africa, but the harp is still played around the world.

One very popular instrument in Europe during the 1500s and 1600s was the lute. Today, lutes come in many different shapes and sizes, but they all have a neck joined to a deep resonating belly.

△ The delicate sound of the harp has often been associated with heavenly matters. This golden statue of King David with a harp is based on a story in the Bible.

△ Irish harps were small and light enough to be carried from town to town by wandering minstrels.

▷ The classical guitar is also known as the Spanish guitar. In the late 1800s, a Spanish guitar maker, Antonio Torres Juardo, created the basic size and shape of the modern guitar. The Spanish guitarist and composer, Francisco Tárrega, developed present-day guitar-playing methods.

Fingerboard

Metal frets

Sound hole allows sound out of the sound chamber

Bridge supports the strings and transmits vibrations to the soundboard

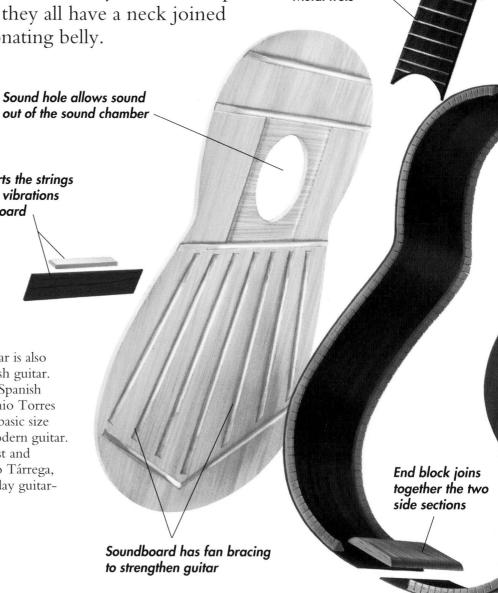

End block joins together the two side sections

Soundboard has fan bracing to strengthen guitar

Tuning head

Nut

Neck

THE EUROPEAN RENAISSANCE LUTE

Throughout the 1500s and 1600s, lute makers aimed to make the instrument as light as possible—consequently the bodies of some lutes were only .04 inches (1mm) thick. Many were beautifully decorated with ebony and ivory.

▽ John Williams (born 1941) is an Australian guitarist who plays both classical and jazz music. He studied with the great Spanish guitarist, Andrés Segovia. In the late 1970s, he formed the rock group, Sky.

Strings made from nylon

Top block joins the neck to the body

Rosewood back

Maker's label

▽ Lyres are still widely played in many African countries, often at religious festivals and in magical rites. This large, box-shaped lyre, called a *beganna*, is found only in Ethopia.

Curved side section

LISTEN FOR

LUTE
John Dowland—
Lachrimae

Johann Sebastian Bach—
Lute Suites

HARP
Wolfgang Amadeus Mozart—
Flute and Harp Concerto

GUITAR
Antonio Vivaldi—
Guitar Concertos in A major and D minor

Manuel De Falla—
Homage for the Tomb of Debussy and *Nights in the Gardens of Spain*

Heitor Villa-Lobos—
Preludes

Zithers and Fiddles

Some of the most beautiful stringed instruments come from India where the tradition of string playing goes back many thousands of years. One of the oldest is the *vina*, a type of zither (an instrument with strings running the entire length of the body). According to Indian legend, the *vina* was first made by the god Krishna in the likeness of the goddess Parvati. Its delicate sound is supposed to echo the softness of her breathing.

Zithers are also important in Japan, China, and other East Asian countries. The shape of the Japanese *koto* is said to have come from the appearance of a crouching dragon. This instrument has 13 silk strings stretched across a wooden sound box. A similar instrument is also played in China, where it is called a *ch'in*, and in Korea, where it is known as a *kayagum*. Board zithers are found throughout Europe. These zithers have strings stretched across a flat or gently curving wooden board.

△ The board zither has been a popular folk instrument in Europe for more than 200 years.

◁ Japan's national instrument is the *koto*. Underneath each of the 13 silk strings is a bridge that can be moved to produce different notes.

Metal strings

Sliding metal rings for fine-tuning

▷ The *vina* has a rounded body carved from wood, with a gourd attached to the hollow neck. This instrument, from southern India, has seven metal strings and 24 brass frets. The strings are plucked with a plectrum, or by long fingernails on the player's right hand.

▷ The Chinese *erhu* is known as the spike fiddle because its long neck pierces the sound box. The bow is threaded through the *erhu's* two strings.

Sound table

Decorated sound hole

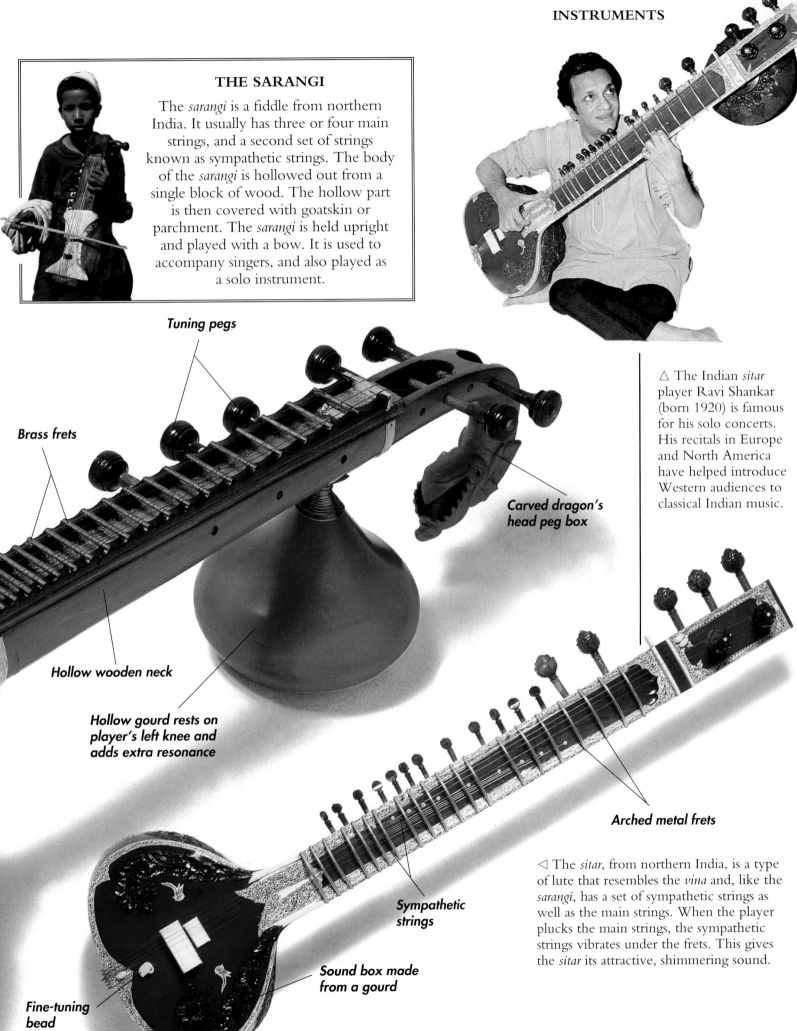

THE SARANGI

The *sarangi* is a fiddle from northern India. It usually has three or four main strings, and a second set of strings known as sympathetic strings. The body of the *sarangi* is hollowed out from a single block of wood. The hollow part is then covered with goatskin or parchment. The *sarangi* is held upright and played with a bow. It is used to accompany singers, and also played as a solo instrument.

Tuning pegs

Brass frets

Carved dragon's head peg box

Hollow wooden neck

Hollow gourd rests on player's left knee and adds extra resonance

△ The Indian *sitar* player Ravi Shankar (born 1920) is famous for his solo concerts. His recitals in Europe and North America have helped introduce Western audiences to classical Indian music.

Arched metal frets

Sympathetic strings

Sound box made from a gourd

Fine-tuning bead

◁ The *sitar*, from northern India, is a type of lute that resembles the *vina* and, like the *sarangi*, has a set of sympathetic strings as well as the main strings. When the player plucks the main strings, the sympathetic strings vibrates under the frets. This gives the *sitar* its attractive, shimmering sound.

71

Orchestral Strings

The violin is one of the most expressive of all instruments and forms the backbone of the Western orchestra. As a solo instrument it is at times sad and soulful, and at other times flamboyant and lively. The sound of many violins played in unison is just as pleasing. The viola is only slightly bigger than the violin, but its tone is deeper and more mellow.

The cello and the double bass form the lower strings in the Western orchestra. Like the violin, the cello's expressive tone makes it an ideal solo instrument. The double bass has its origins in another family of bowed string instruments, the viols, from which it was developed in the 1500s. Measuring 6 feet (1.8 m) in length, it can be played by plucking the strings, as well as by using the bow.

△ The classical string quartet dates from the late 1700s, when both Haydn and Mozart wrote music to be played informally in people's homes. This is why it is sometimes called chamber music. A classical quartet consists of two violins, a viola, and a cello.

▷ Played in Europe during the 1600s and 1700s, the *tromba marina* had only one gut string. The player drew a bow across the top of the instrument, while varying the pitch by stopping the string.

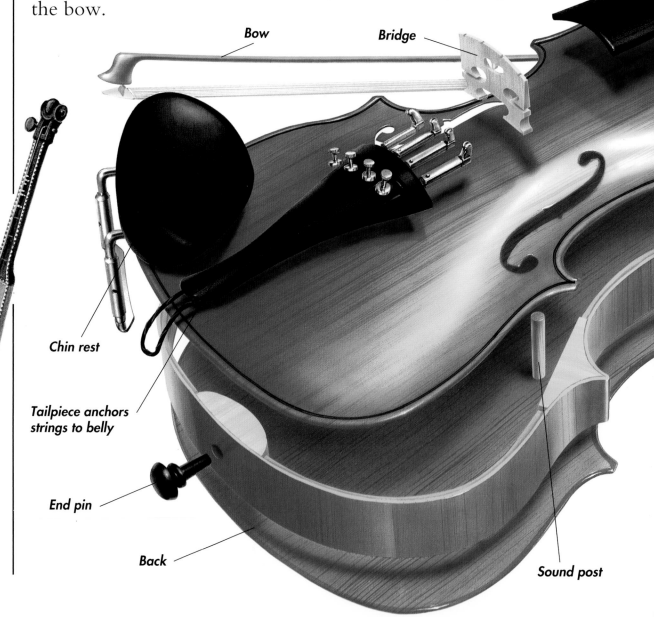

Bow

Bridge

Chin rest

Tailpiece anchors strings to belly

End pin

Back

Sound post

◁ The rock 'n' roll music of Bill Haley and the Comets in the mid–1950s featured a double bass played in an unusual way!

Strings made of metal, or gut wound with thin wire

Peg box

Scroll

Tuning peg

Fingerboard

Horsehair

◁ The modern violin has more than 70 different parts. Its design is both practical and beautiful. The body resonates the sound, while the narrowing, or waist, at the center allows the player to reach the highest and lowest strings.

THE STRING FAMILY

violin

cello

viola

double bass

double bass   cello   viola   violin

LISTEN FOR

VIOLIN
Antonio Vivaldi—
The Four Seasons

Johann Sebastian Bach—
Violin Partita no. 3 in E

Ralph Vaughan Williams
—*The Lark Ascending*

VIOLA
Hector Berlioz—
Harold in Italy

CELLO
Pyotr Ilyich Tchaikovsky—
Variations on a Rococo Theme

Julian Lloyd Webber—
Variations (on a theme of Paganini)

DOUBLE BASS
Camille Saint-Saëns—
Carnival of the Animals (The Elephant)

△ Yehudi Menuhin (born 1916) is one of this century's most celebrated violinists. He was only 16 years old when he made a famous recording of Elgar's *Violin Concerto*, with the composer conducting.

◁ The modern design of the cello was established by Antonio Stradivari in the late 1600s.

Flutes and Recorders

Flutes come in all shapes and sizes, can be made from a number of materials, and produce a wide variety of sounds. The haunting whisper of the panpipes is very different from the clear, liquid tones of the orchestral flute. Different still is the simple and unadorned sound of the recorder. Flutes can be found in many forms around the world. There are bamboo flutes in Asia, clay flutes in South America, and the orchestral flute in the West. The way a flute is played also varies from one instrument to the next—air can be blown down or across the mouthpiece. Some flutes are even played by blowing through the nose!

The orchestral flute is held sideways, is blown across the mouthpiece, and is usually made from metal. The recorder is played downward and has open holes that are covered by the player's fingers. Both these instruments have long histories in the West.

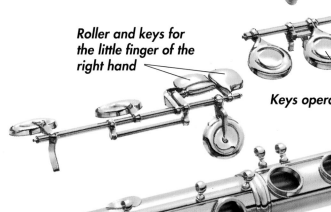

△ The panpipes get their name from the ancient Greek god Pan. It was said that Pan was in love with a nymph who, to escape his advances, was changed into a reed. From this reed, Pan made the first panpipes.

Trill keys

Roller and keys for the little finger of the right hand

Keys operated by fingers

Body joint

Hole covered by key

Foot joint

◁ Unusual and beautiful clay whistles were used over a thousand years ago by the peoples of South America. These were often given the form of animals or people.

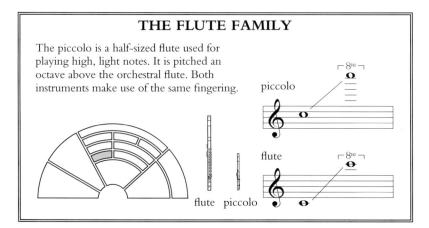

THE FLUTE FAMILY

The piccolo is a half-sized flute used for playing high, light notes. It is pitched an octave above the orchestral flute. Both instruments make use of the same fingering.

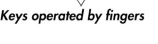

piccolo

flute

flute   piccolo

◁ Some of the peoples who live in the Amazon rain forest believe that air blown through the nose has magical powers. Nose flutes are also common throughout many Pacific islands.

Rod mechanism

Lip plate

▽ The modern orchestral flute dates from the 1840s, when German inventor Theobald Boehm changed its shape and system of keys. Most modern flutes are made from metal, but a few players still use wooden flutes.

△ The Irish flautist James Galway (born 1939) is famed for his fine playing and best-selling records. Before beginning his solo career in 1973, he was the principal flautist with the Berlin Philharmonic Orchestra.

Felt or leather pad under each key makes airtight seal with hole

Screw end for fine tuning

Oval-shaped blow hole

Head joint

DOLMETSCH RECORDER

The recorder was very popular in Europe in the 1500s and 1600s. It was then almost forgotten until the early 1900s, when instrument-maker Arnold Dolmetsch became interested in it. Through an accident, his own recorder was lost. Luckily, he had taken careful measurements and based a new instrument on the old design! This was the beginning of a revival for the recorder.

MUSICAL SPY

The *shakuhachi* is an end-blown bamboo flute from Japan, with five finger holes. Traditionally, many *shakuhachi* players were priests who wore a kind of wickerwork basket over their heads while they played. It is said that these priests were actually spies working for a secret group. Their identity hidden, they walked the city streets eavesdropping on interesting conversations while playing soft tunes on the *shakuhachi*.

LISTEN FOR

RECORDER
The recorder features in many Baroque works by Antonio Vivaldi, Alessandro Scarlatti, and George Philipp Telemann

FLUTE
Johann Sebastian Bach—
Suite no. 2 in B minor

Wolfgang Amadeus Mozart—
Flute Concerto in G major

Gabriel Fauré—
Fantaisie

Claude Debussy—
Syrinx

Paul Hindemith –
Sonata for flute and piano

PICCOLO
Benjamin Britten—
Variations on a theme by Purcell

Oboes and Clarinets

The oboe and the clarinet are both instruments that use reeds to create air vibrations. The main difference between them is that the oboe has two reeds that vibrate together (a double reed), while the clarinet has a single reed. The oboe has an unmistakable, mournful tone. Its tone is so clear that it plays the note to which all the other members of the orchestra tune their instruments. The clarinet has a smoother, more velvety sound.

Like the flute, relations of the oboe and clarinet are found all over the world. The *shawm* is an ancient double-reed instrument with a loud, shrill sound that is often played at outdoor events. Folk clarinets from the side-blown *bumpa* of Burkina Faso, formerly known as Upper Volta, now named to the cane clarinets of South America have also been played for thousands of years.

△ The clarinet, in a variety of forms, has been a popular folk instrument for thousands of years in many different cultures.

CLARINETS

The bass clarinet is twice as long as the normal clarinet, and it plays notes an octave lower. The top part of the instrument curves over to make it easier to play.

clarinet

bass clarinet

clarinet   bass clarinet

△ The *shawm* is a type of ancient folk oboe found throughout parts of Europe, Asia, and Africa. The round metal plate below the mouthpiece supports the player's lips.

Key

Keys for right hand on middle joint

Lower joint

Flared bell projects sound outward

Keys for little finger of right hand

△ A type of clarinet was first played in ancient Egypt. The instrument we play today was developed in the 1700s by J. C. Denner of Germany.

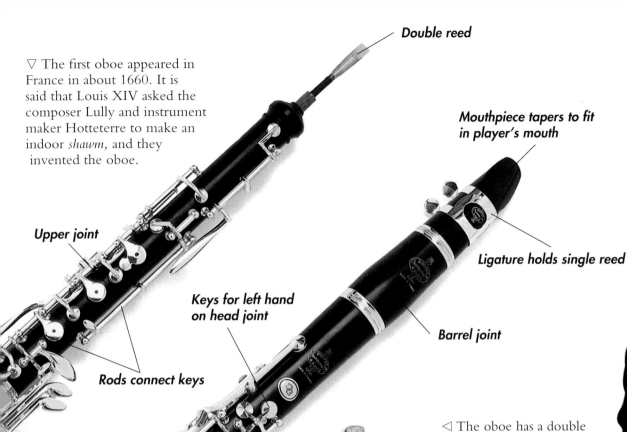

Double reed

▽ The first oboe appeared in France in about 1660. It is said that Louis XIV asked the composer Lully and instrument maker Hotteterre to make an indoor *shawm*, and they invented the oboe.

Upper joint

Keys for left hand on head joint

Rods connect keys

Keys for little finger of left hand

Mouthpiece tapers to fit in player's mouth

Ligature holds single reed

Barrel joint

◁ The oboe has a double reed *(left)* that is placed onto a staple, or metal tube. Cork surrounds the staple to make sure of a tight fit. Many oboists make their own reeds, carefully scraping the cane until it is exactly the right shape. The clarinet has a single reed *(right)* that slots into the mouthpiece. A metal band holds the reed in place.

▽ Heinz Holliger (born 1939) is a Swiss oboist and composer who is well known for his experimental work on the oboe. He has pioneered different techniques to achieve new sounds and effects.

OBOE FAMILY

The cor anglais is the tenor version of the oboe. It has a deep plaintive tone. The bassoon has a long conical tube (about ten feet long) that doubles back on itself.

oboe

cor anglais

bassoon

oboe   cor anglais   bassoon

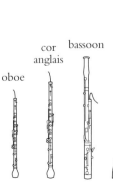

▽ Benny Goodman (1909–1986), a clarinetist, was famous for playing both jazz and classical music. He commissioned Copland's *Clarinet Concerto,* first performed in 1950.

LISTEN FOR

OBOE
George Frideric Handel—
Arrival of the Queen of Sheba

Ludwig van Beethoven—
Symphony no. 6 "Pastoral"

Edvard Grieg—
Peer Gynt "Morning"

Sergei Prokofiev—
Peter and the Wolf

CLARINET
Wolfgang Amadeus Mozart—
Clarinet Quintet

Carl Maria von Weber—
Der Freischütz

Igor Stravinsky—
Ebony Concerto

Aaron Copland—
Concerto for clarinet, harp, and strings

George Gershwin—
Rhapsody in Blue

Saxophones and Bagpipes

The saxophone was invented in the early 1840s by an instrument-maker named Adophe Sax. A cross between a woodwind and a brass instrument, it was originally intended for use in military and marching bands. Today, its highly expressive sound is associated most often with jazz music. Although it makes an occasional appearance in the Western orchestra, the saxophone has never become a regular member of the woodwind or brass section.

The bagpipe has a much longer history than the saxophone, dating back some 3,000 years. When the player squeezes the bag, air is pushed out through one or more pipes attached to the bag. Inside the pipes are reeds, which vibrate as the air flows over them. This gives the bagpipe its very distinctive, raucous sound.

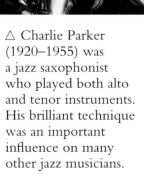

△ Traditionally, the bagpipe was played by shepherds and other rural dwellers. This woodcarving from the 1400s shows a French piper.

Single reed mouthpiece

▷ The saxophone has a metal body, the mouthpiece of a clarinet, and a flared bell. An accomplished player can make this eloquent instrument sound loud or soft, harsh or smooth.

Rod mechanism connects keys to pads

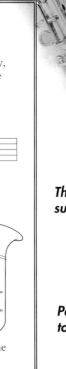

Key

Bell

Thumb support

Pads close tone holes

Melody pipe, or chanter

△ Charlie Parker (1920–1955) was a jazz saxophonist who played both alto and tenor instruments. His brilliant technique was an important influence on many other jazz musicians.

THE SAXOPHONE FAMILY

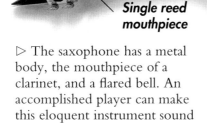

Originally there were 14 different members of the saxophone family. Today, only four saxophones are used regularly.

soprano

alto   baritone

tenor

soprano   alto   tenor   baritone

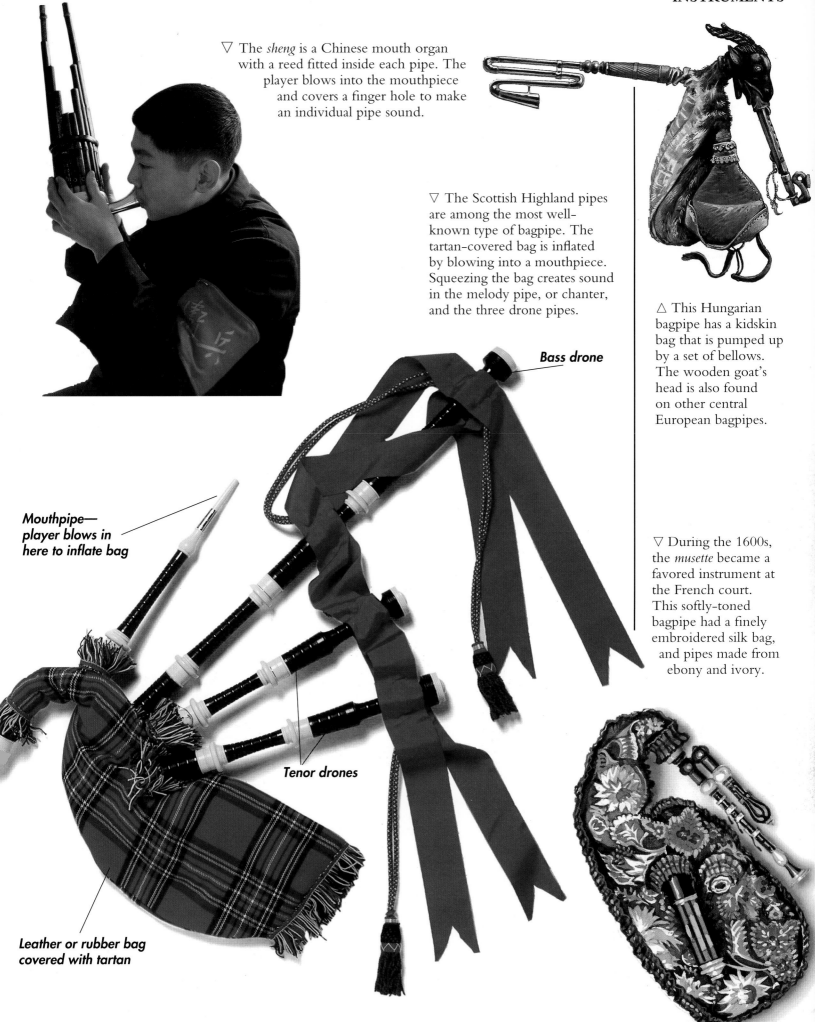

▽ The *sheng* is a Chinese mouth organ with a reed fitted inside each pipe. The player blows into the mouthpiece and covers a finger hole to make an individual pipe sound.

▽ The Scottish Highland pipes are among the most well-known type of bagpipe. The tartan-covered bag is inflated by blowing into a mouthpiece. Squeezing the bag creates sound in the melody pipe, or chanter, and the three drone pipes.

△ This Hungarian bagpipe has a kidskin bag that is pumped up by a set of bellows. The wooden goat's head is also found on other central European bagpipes.

▽ During the 1600s, the *musette* became a favored instrument at the French court. This softly-toned bagpipe had a finely embroidered silk bag, and pipes made from ebony and ivory.

Bass drone

**Mouthpipe—
player blows in
here to inflate bag**

Tenor drones

**Leather or rubber bag
covered with tartan**

Horns—Ancient and Modern

△ A hunting scene depicted in a French book of the 1400s. French hunting horns were wide enough for the huntsman to wear the horn over his shoulders.

The first horns were made from animal horn. By breaking off the horn's tip and blowing down the hole, a note could be sounded. Further holes were sometimes drilled into the side of the horn. These were covered and uncovered by the player's fingers to make extra notes. Some early horns were used in Medieval Europe as signaling instruments, especially for hunting. When composers such as Lully wrote hunting scenes in their operas, they included the horn's familiar call, which effectively introduced the horn into the orchestra. By the late 1700s, Mozart was writing concertos for the solo horn and orchestra.

During the 1800s, the horn acquired valves, which made the instrument easier to play. At the beginning of the l900s the double, or French, horn was developed and it has since become a standard member of the orchestra.

FRENCH HORN

The horn is pitched in F and is capable of playing just over two octaves—from F in the bass clef, up to C in the treble clef. In the orchestra, the horn is positioned next to the trumpets and behind the clarinets.

Wide flaring bell— hand is inserted to adjust pitch and support instrument

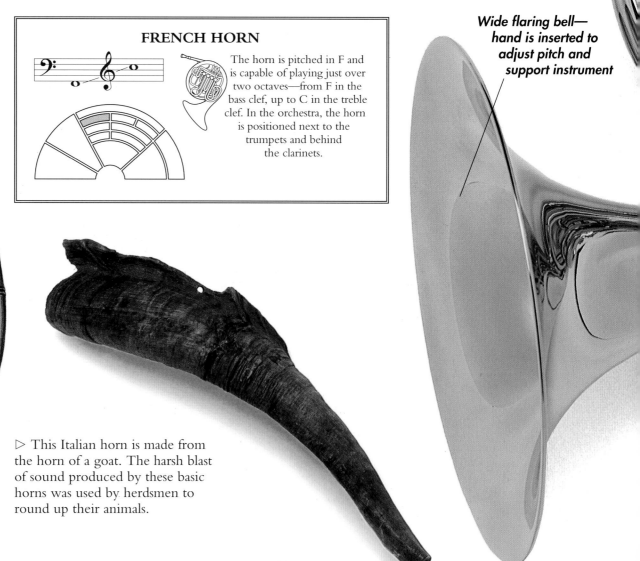

▷ The lur is a Bronze Age horn found in Scandinavia. Its shape is thought to be based upon a mammoth's horn.

▷ This Italian horn is made from the horn of a goat. The harsh blast of sound produced by these basic horns was used by herdsmen to round up their animals.

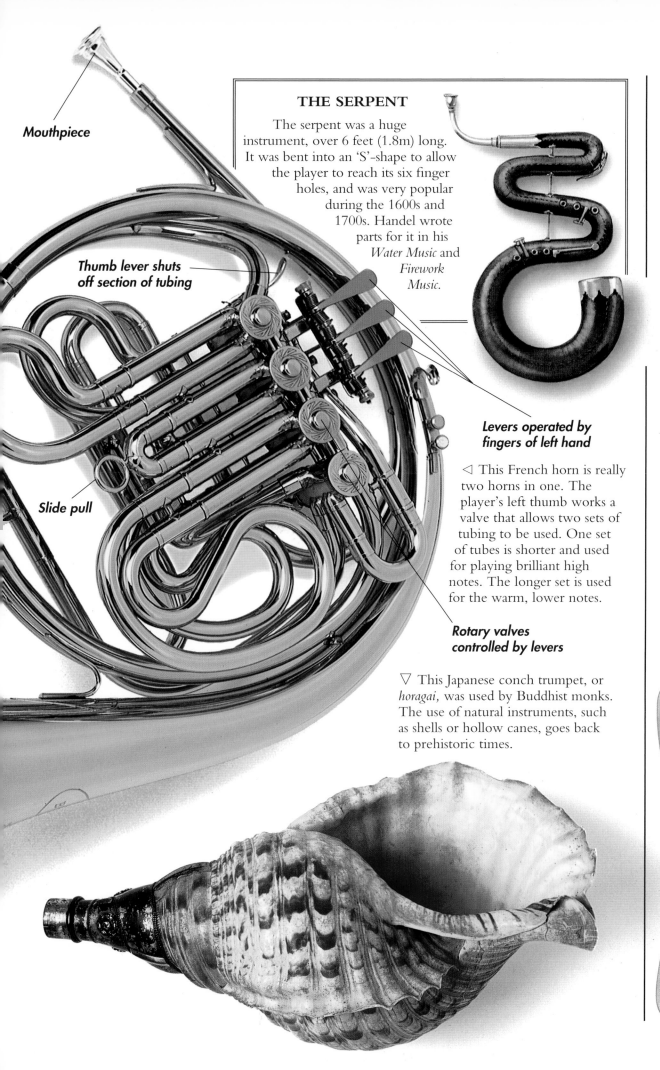

Mouthpiece

Thumb lever shuts off section of tubing

Slide pull

THE SERPENT

The serpent was a huge instrument, over 6 feet (1.8m) long. It was bent into an 'S'-shape to allow the player to reach its six finger holes, and was very popular during the 1600s and 1700s. Handel wrote parts for it in his *Water Music* and *Firework Music*.

Levers operated by fingers of left hand

◁ This French horn is really two horns in one. The player's left thumb works a valve that allows two sets of tubing to be used. One set of tubes is shorter and used for playing brilliant high notes. The longer set is used for the warm, lower notes.

Rotary valves controlled by levers

▽ This Japanese conch trumpet, or *horagai*, was used by Buddhist monks. The use of natural instruments, such as shells or hollow canes, goes back to prehistoric times.

▽ Barry Tuckwell, born in 1931. An Australian French horn player, he was principal horn with the London Symphony Orchestra, 1955–1968. Well known as a soloist, composers such as Thea Musgrave have written works for him.

LISTEN FOR

HORN

Johann Sebastian Bach—
The Brandenburg Concertos

Wolfgang Amadeus Mozart—
Concerto no.1 in D Major

Robert Alexander Schumann
Conzertstück

Benjamin Britten—
Serenade for Tenor, Horn and Strings

Felix Mendelssohn—
A Midsummer Night's Dream

Pyotr Ilyich Tchaikovsky—
Symphony no.5 (slow movement)

George Frideric Handel—
Water Music

Claude Debussy—
La Mer

Trombones and Trumpets

The shrill sound of the trumpet has long been used to send signals and messages, to frighten enemies in battle, and to celebrate rituals and ceremonies. The sound of conch shell trumpets was heard by Captain Cook as he approached the islands of Hawaii in the Pacific. The islanders were trying to scare off his ships with their wild noises! The Romans also knew the value of the trumpet—especially in war. They used a long trumpet called a *cornu* both to direct the movements of their own troops and to strike fear in the enemy.

The trombone first appears in European paintings from about 1460. Early trombones in England were known as sackbuts. Apart from a wider tube and a different mouthpiece, the trombone has changed very little over the centuries. Today, the trombone has a regular place in marching bands, orchestras, and in jazz music.

△ A wooden angel trumpeter outside St. David's Cathedral, in Wales.

Flared bell

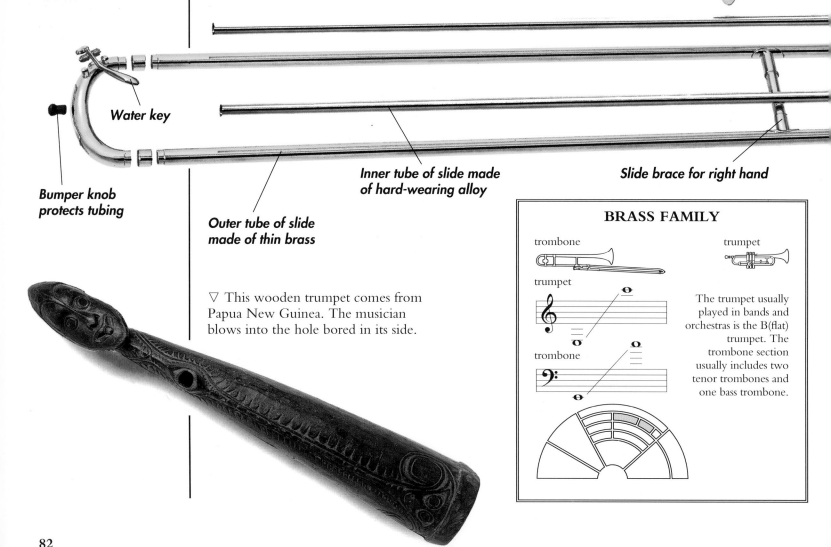

Water key

Bumper knob protects tubing

Outer tube of slide made of thin brass

Inner tube of slide made of hard-wearing alloy

Slide brace for right hand

▽ This wooden trumpet comes from Papua New Guinea. The musician blows into the hole bored in its side.

BRASS FAMILY

trombone   trumpet

trumpet

trombone

The trumpet usually played in bands and orchestras is the B(flat) trumpet. The trombone section usually includes two tenor trombones and one bass trombone.

LISTEN FOR

TRUMPET
Joseph Haydn—
Trumpet Concerto

Antonio Vivaldi—
Trumpet Concerto

George Gershwin—
An American in Paris

Miles Davis—
Kind of Blue

TROMBONE
Richard Wagner—
Overture Tannhäuser

Luciano Berio—
Sequenza V

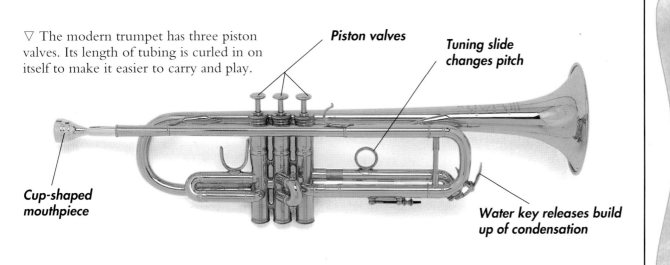

▽ The modern trumpet has three piston valves. Its length of tubing is curled in on itself to make it easier to carry and play.

Piston valves

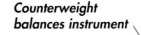

Tuning slide changes pitch

Cup-shaped mouthpiece

Water key releases build up of condensation

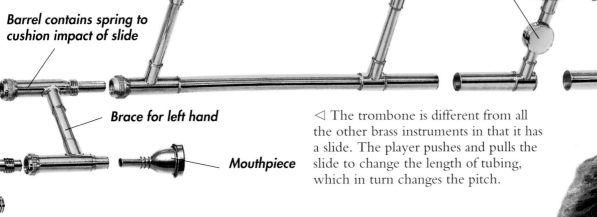

Counterweight balances instrument

Tuning slide bow

Barrel contains spring to cushion impact of slide

Brace for left hand

Mouthpiece

◁ The trombone is different from all the other brass instruments in that it has a slide. The player pushes and pulls the slide to change the length of tubing, which in turn changes the pitch.

▽ Trumpeter Miles Davis (1926-1991) was one of the most inventive jazz musicians of all time. He developed bebop and jazz fusion, which combined jazz with rock.

◁ The didgeridoo makes a deep, droning sound and is played by the Aborigine people of Australia. The player must breathe in through the nose while blowing down the hollowed out instrument.

Tubas and Bugles

The tuba plays the deepest and the weightiest notes in the brass section of the Western orchestra, and is this section's youngest member. The tuba was first used in military bands in Berlin in the 1830s, only taking its place in the orchestra in the later 1800s. Composers such as Richard Wagner began to use it to add extra power to the bass line. During this period, makers of instruments experimented with many different designs. Perhaps the best known of these instruments is the sousaphone—a bass tuba with a huge bell. Today, the tuba is still an important member of military bands in Europe and the United States. It is often simply referred to as the "bass."

△ The English Coldstream Guards' band on parade. The bold, rousing sound of the tuba and trombone makes them ideally suited to military or marching bands.

Piston valves open and shut tubing

◁ The cornet is played in the same way as the trumpet, but it makes a more mellow, rounded sound. It is the lead instrument in brass bands.

△ In the 1870s, the composer Richard Wagner developed an instrument called a Wagner tuba. Its sound bridged the gap between that of the French horn and the trombone.

THE BUGLE

The bugle has been a military instrument since the late 1700s, when it was used to send signals in battle and during the army's normal daily routine. The bugle is a small instrument that can be held in one hand as it is played. Military bugles are often decorated with tasseled cords.

Large flaring bell amplifies sound

◁ The tuba is both an orchestral and a band instrument. In the orchestra it is held on the player's lap. For marching in a military band, the tuba is rested on the player's shoulder.

Wide bore gives deep and smooth sound

Cup-shaped mouthpiece

◁ The sousaphone was built in the 1800s for the composer, John Philip Sousa. The bell can be made from fiberglass to reduce weight and make marching with it easier.

◁ Despite its large size, the tuba can produce a surprisingly agile sound. It is normally used, however, to add weight to the bass line in the orchestra, where it can be heard to play its distinctive oom-pah-pahs!

▽ The inspiring Swedish tuba player, Michael Lind, is director of the first Scandinavian Brass Symposium.

Slide pull-ring adjusts pitch

THE TUBA

There are five different sizes of tuba ranging from the euphonium to the contrabass tuba. The orchestral tuba is the most common. Tubas sit next to the trombone section in the orchestra.

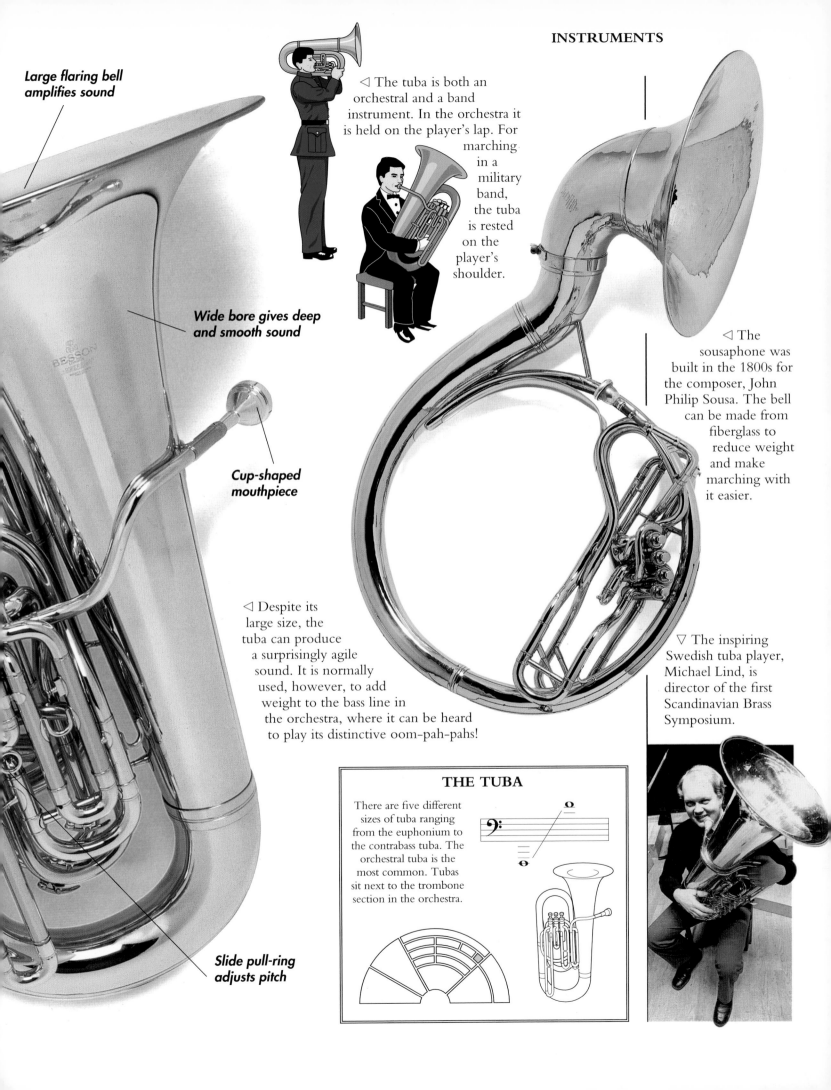

Keyboard Instruments

Invented over 2,000 years ago, the organ is unique among keyboard instruments. While the strings of the harpsichord are plucked, and those of the piano are struck, the organ is powered by wind. Compressed air flows along its pipes, giving the organ its rich, resonating sound. Depending on the row of pipes played, however, its tones may be reedy or flutelike.

The most important of the keyboard instruments during the Baroque and Classical periods was the harpsichord, with its bright, clear sound. It lost some popularity after the 1700s when the pianoforte (or piano) became more well known. Bartolommeo Cristofori, the piano's inventor, called it a "harpsichord with loud and soft." The piano's response to the touch of the finger creates great expression and a "singing" quality. Its full potential began to be realized from the 1770s, when Mozart started to play and compose for it.

Two keyboards, or manuals

△ In this painting from the 1400s, an angel plays a portative organ. The bellows of this small, portable instrument were worked by the player's left hand.

▽ The organ is often called the "king of instruments" because many examples are so large. The two great eras of organ building took place in northern Germany during the 1600s, and France during the 1800s.

Television monitor allows organist to see conductor's beat

Stops

Set of five manuals

◁ The organ in Westminster Abbey has five manuals, or keyboards, and over 120 stops. When a stop is pulled out it allows air to flow through a specific set of pipes. Like all modern organs, it is powered by electricity.

Swell pedals control volume of sound

Pedal board operated by player's feet

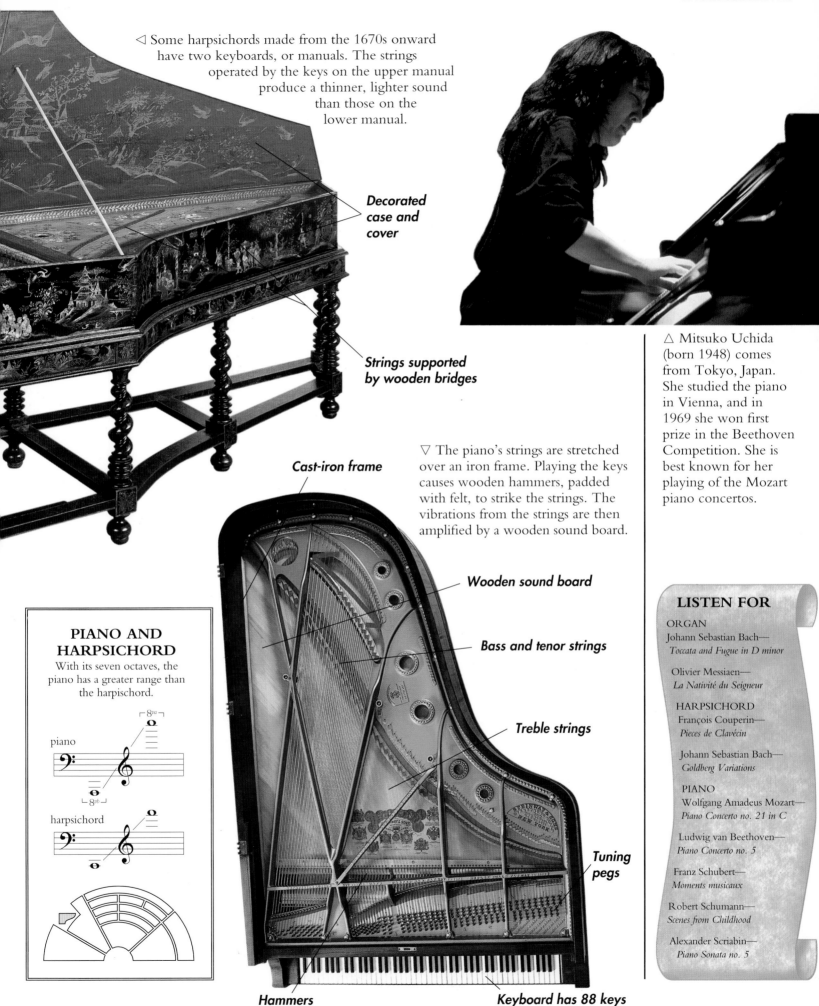

◁ Some harpsichords made from the 1670s onward have two keyboards, or manuals. The strings operated by the keys on the upper manual produce a thinner, lighter sound than those on the lower manual.

Decorated case and cover

Strings supported by wooden bridges

△ Mitsuko Uchida (born 1948) comes from Tokyo, Japan. She studied the piano in Vienna, and in 1969 she won first prize in the Beethoven Competition. She is best known for her playing of the Mozart piano concertos.

▽ The piano's strings are stretched over an iron frame. Playing the keys causes wooden hammers, padded with felt, to strike the strings. The vibrations from the strings are then amplified by a wooden sound board.

Cast-iron frame

Wooden sound board

Bass and tenor strings

Treble strings

Tuning pegs

Hammers

Keyboard has 88 keys

PIANO AND HARPSICHORD

With its seven octaves, the piano has a greater range than the harpsichord.

piano

harpsichord

LISTEN FOR

ORGAN
Johann Sebastian Bach—
Toccata and Fugue in D minor

Olivier Messiaen—
La Nativité du Seigneur

HARPSICHORD
François Couperin—
Pieces de Clavécin

Johann Sebastian Bach—
Goldberg Variations

PIANO
Wolfgang Amadeus Mozart—
Piano Concerto no. 21 in C

Ludwig van Beethoven—
Piano Concerto no. 5

Franz Schubert—
Moments musicaux

Robert Schumann—
Scenes from Childhood

Alexander Scriabin—
Piano Sonata no. 5

Electronic Instruments

▽ Invented in the 1920s, the ondes martenot is played from a keyboard, or by sliding a metal ring along a track. It makes a weird, swooping sound.

Ever since the early years of the 1900s, new instruments have been developed in step with the latest technology. The discovery that air vibrations can be turned into electrical signals has led to the invention of all kinds of musical instruments. These range from the rarely heard theremin and ondes martenot to the hugely popular electric guitar, which was developed in the 1950s. The synthesizer, which first appeared in the 1960s, revolutionized electronic music by allowing musicians to create totally new sounds.

Today, one of the most exciting areas of music making lies with the computer. Although the computer itself is not a musical instrument, synthesizers, samplers, and sequencers can be connected to it to allow the creation of an endless variety of musical sounds and effects.

Pitch wheel

▽ The spooky sound of the theremin is controlled by the position of the player's hands. The instrument was named after its Russian inventor, Leon Theremin.

Solid wooden body

Strap screw

Bridge

Fingerplate

Tremolo arm varies pitch

Output socket to amplifier

Control knobs

Pickups turn vibrations into electric signals

Back panel contains MIDI and stereo output connections

Display panel

Pre-set and edit buttons control stored sounds and create new ones

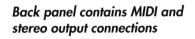
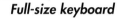

◁ The modern synthesizer can reproduce the sound of any instrument or create entirely new ones. The sounds are made by special circuits called oscillators and shaped by other circuits called filters.

Full-size keyboard

▽ The electric guitar has a flat, solid body. Unlike an acoustic guitar, there is no need for a resonator because the vibrations of the strings are picked up and amplified electronically. This guitar is commonly used in rock bands.

Tuning head

Metal frets

Fingerboard

Fret position markers

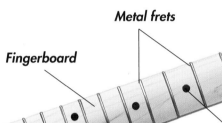

Steel strings

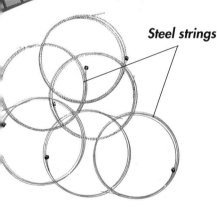

△ Jimi Hendrix (1942–1970) was a rock musician. He dazzled audiences with his inspired playing of the electric guitar.

SEMI-ACOUSTIC

The semi-acoustic guitar is a cross between an acoustic guitar and an electric guitar. It has electric pickups and a hollow, resonating body. This allows the guitarist to play with or without amplification.

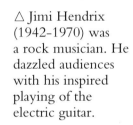

▷ Traditional instruments, as well as synthesizers, can be connected to a computer using a MIDI (Musical Instrument Digital Interface) lead. Once stored in the computer's memory, the musical sounds can be triggered to produce a whole range of different effects.

LISTEN FOR

ELECTRIC GUITAR
Jimi Hendrix—*Purple Haze*

Eric Clapton—*Layla*

Peter Green—*Albatross*

Prince—*Purple Rain*

ONDES MARTENOT
Olivier Messiaen—
Turangalîla-symphonie

THEREMIN
The Beach Boys—
Good Vibrations

SYNTHESIZER
Jean-Michel Jarre—
Oxygène

Kraftwerk—*The Model*

Playing as a Team

For many people music is a communal activity, whether it is played by a local band or grand symphony orchestra. Being part of a group has its own rewards, but some of the wonder of playing music in a team is that its beauty can be enriched with a range of voices or instruments. The first Western orchestras accompanied singers and consisted only of stringed instruments. The orchestra only really came into its own in the 1700s, when pieces were written especially for it. The new symphonies demanded a greater number of players, leading to the introduction of a conductor to hold everyone together. Even today, however, small orchestras can still be directed by the lead violin.

△ A gathering of musical ladies and gentlemen in the 1700s. This kind of music making was popular among the merchant and aristocratic classes.

▽ The conductor interprets the music, deciding on such things as beat, "phrasing," and tempo. Most conductors use a baton to direct the orchestra.

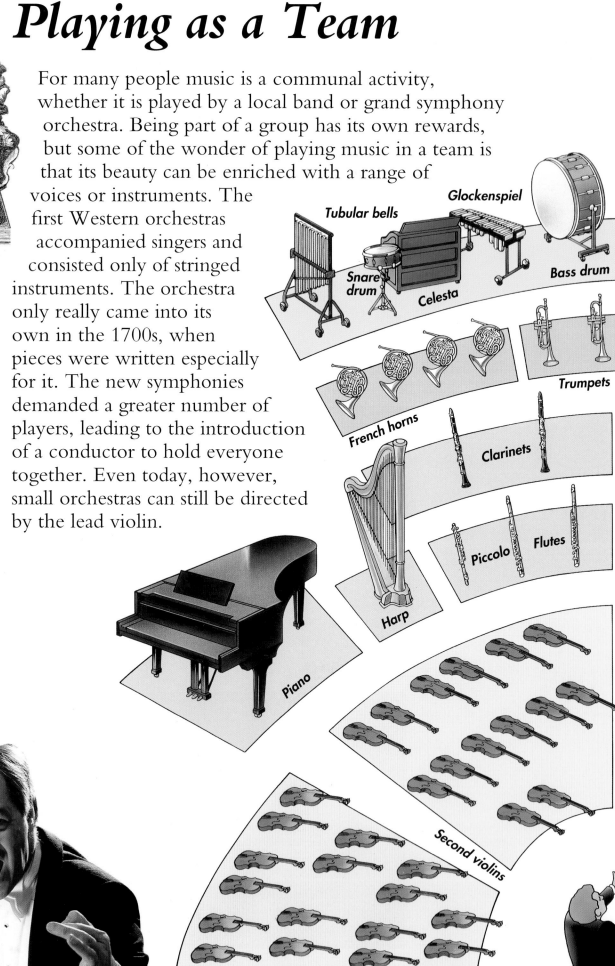

Tubular bells

Glockenspiel

Snare drum

Celesta

Bass drum

French horns

Trumpets

Clarinets

Harp

Piccolo

Flutes

Piano

Second violins

First violins

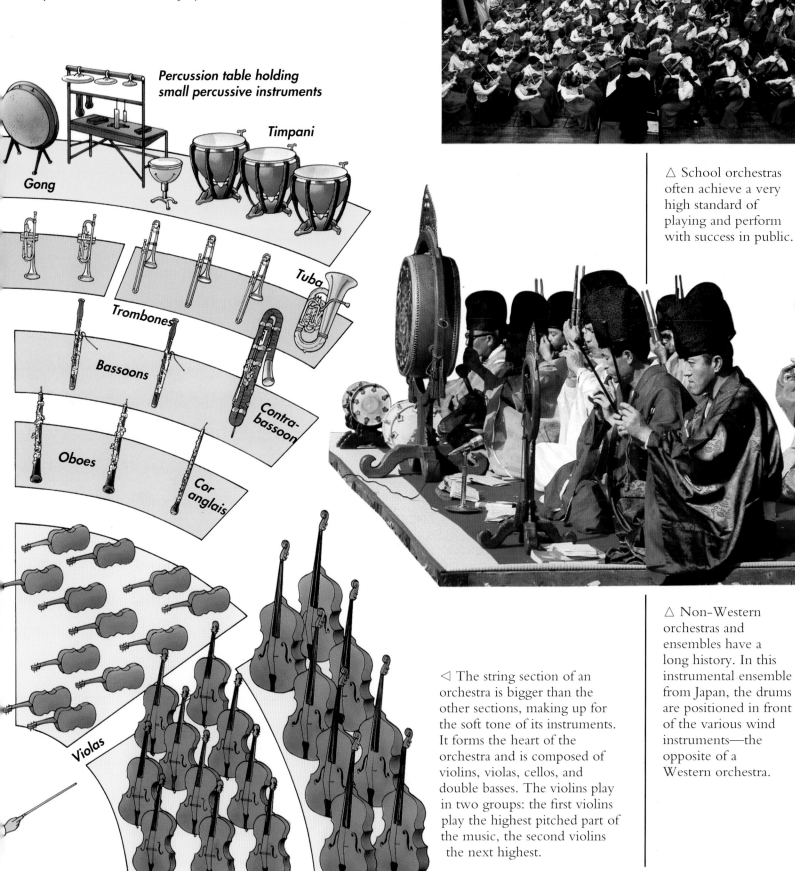

▽ A typical orchestra is made up of about twenty different kinds of instrument, which are divided into four main sections—strings, woodwind, brass, and percussion. A very large symphony orchestra may have over a hundred players.

Percussion table holding small percussive instruments

Gong

Timpani

Tuba

Trombones

Bassoons

Contra-bassoon

Oboes

Cor anglais

Violas

Cellos

Double basses

△ School orchestras often achieve a very high standard of playing and perform with success in public.

△ Non-Western orchestras and ensembles have a long history. In this instrumental ensemble from Japan, the drums are positioned in front of the various wind instruments—the opposite of a Western orchestra.

◁ The string section of an orchestra is bigger than the other sections, making up for the soft tone of its instruments. It forms the heart of the orchestra and is composed of violins, violas, cellos, and double basses. The violins play in two groups: the first violins play the highest pitched part of the music, the second violins the next highest.

Amateur Music Making

All over the world there are talented musicians— performing formally or informally, by themselves or in groups—who make music just for the love of it. Such musicians are known as amateurs. Unlike their professional counterparts who earn a living through their art, amateur musicians are able to play for sheer pleasure. Some amateurs, however, rank among the world's best musicians. The London Bach Choir, for example, sings alongside top professional orchestras.

Other amateurs take a more low-key approach. They are happy to sing or play in town halls or squares, or in bars and cafés. Many schools and youth groups encourage young talent by putting on their own musical performances, while local music competitions are popular with both young and older amateurs.

Street musicians cross the boundaries between amateur and professional. The magic of an unexpected tune played by a musician can brighten up a gloomy city street. Even the busy commuter might stop and listen for a while, showing his or her pleasure by giving money.

△ A mother teaches her son to play the hurdy-gurdy. Traditionally, musical skills were handed down the generations from parent to child.

▷ Students playing in a string quartet bring music to a busy street in Dublin, Ireland. Onlookers show their appreciation by dropping money into the open cello case.

FAMOUS AMATEURS

Prince Albert plays the harmonium to Queen Victoria and the German composer Felix Mendelssohn. Other gifted amateurs with royal connections include King David in the Old Testament, King Henry VIII of England, and Frederick the Great of Prussia. Among nonroyal amateurs, the Russian scientist and composer Alexander Borodin is one of the most well known.

△ A young African boy strums a home-made guitar while listening to music on his personal stereo.

◁ The Japanese violinist Shinichi Suzuki believed that the best way for young people to learn an instrument is to play together. Today, thousands of children learn to play the violin using the Suzuki method.

93

The Power of Music

△ In ancient Egypt music was important for entertainment and religious ritual. Here, musicians entertain guests at a banquet. One plays a flute while the other claps.

Music is such a powerful force that, according to many legends, it was created by the gods themselves. An Ancient Greek myth tells how Orpheus was given the gift of music by the gods. He played his lyre so beautifully that he could charm the trees, the mountains, and even the wild beasts with his music. While such myths celebrate the heavenly origins of sound, other myths celebrate music as a creative force. A Polynesian chant relates how the world was created through the songs of the god Taaroa.

In the past, people often called upon the strength of music to aid them in their everyday lives. There are work songs for all times of the farming year, as well as songs sung by shepherds or cowherds to their animals. Sometimes, though, work songs had a more practical purpose. At sea, for example, sailors heaving on a rope sang in rhythm to help them pull together. These work songs are known as chanteys.

In some cultures, music has traditionally been used to treat and relieve distress and illness. Music therapy, in which music is played or listened to as part of the healing process, is now becoming more common in modern medicine.

◁ A sailor dances the hornpipe to the accompaniment of a violin. As well as enjoying music and dances in their free time, sailors also had a range of songs to help them while they worked on board ship.

◁ Shamans, or witch doctors, use the energy of music and dance to enter a trancelike state. Shamans believe that in this state they are able to bring some of the powers from the spirit world to the human one.

MUSIC THERAPY

Music therapy is a way of using music to help people. Here, a child with disabilities explores his feelings through the experience of playing a drum.

People who have difficulty communicating in words often find that they can express themselves more freely by making music. This can help them to cope more effectively with their everyday lives.

▷ A Dinka man from southern Sudan bangs a slit drum while telling a story. In many cultures, stories are accompanied by music making.

Dance

Dancing is one of the oldest and most expressive forms of communication. Since the earliest times, dance, like music, has been closely linked to the rhythms of everyday life. Through sound and movement, early peoples praised their gods and tried to understand the world around them. The major events of life—birth, death, the changing of the seasons, the coming of spring, seedtime, and harvest—were all celebrated by ritual dancing. There were also dances for special occasions, such as when war broke out, a successful hunt, or praying to the gods for rain.

In some cultures, ritual dances continue to play a very important part. In Europe, people still perform dances, such as the Maypole celebration, which have their origins in traditions that are thousands of years old.

All around the world people dance for pleasure. Ballroom dances such as the waltz, the fox trot, tap, and many Latin American dances have specific steps and rhythms. Other dances have a much freer range of movements. Dancing can also be used to tell stories. In India, many dances act out legends, myths, and historical events. Classical ballet, too, is based on storytelling as are the Japanese dance dramas, *no* and *kabuki*.

△ The Hindu god, Shiva, performs the dance of creation and destruction at the center of the universe. Shiva is also known as Sri Nataraja, Lord of the Dance.

◁ The tradition of Maypole dancing still continues in parts of Europe. The origin of the Maypole is thought to be the mythical Tree of Life that linked Earth with heaven and the gods above. The dance was originally part of a spring fertility ritual, to secure healthy crops and a good harvest later in the year.

◁ The leopard dance is a ceremonial hunting dance of the Bapende people of Zaire. Their masks and costumes symbolize the leopard.

◁ Modern dance has done away with many of the postures and traditions of classical ballet. Often, a modern dance does not relate a particular story, but aims to evoke a certain mood or feeling.

CLASSICAL BALLET

The styles and traditions of ballet grew out of the dances of the European courts, beginning in Italy in the 1400s. Classical ballet dancers learned to keep their bodies still while extending their arms and legs in elegant, formal movements. In the 1800s, many ballets told stories of delicate, make-believe creatures. Dancers depicted these with quick, light movements performed on tiptoe. The scene below comes from the classical ballet, *Swan Lake*, whose music was composed by Pyotr Ilyich Tchaikovsky. Through their expressive movements, the dancers tell the story of Prince Siegfried, Odile, and Odette—the Swan Princess.

The Music Industry

△ The program for an 1814 performance in Vienna of *Fidelio*, Beethoven's only opera.

▽ Performers such as the Irish band U2 require an army of assistants to organize publicity, travel, and security when they are on tour.

Music is for enjoyment, but it is also one of the biggest industries in the world and makes billions of dollars a year. It needs writers, performers, administrators, and manufacturers to supply and run it. Composers earn money when their music is played, musicians and record companies make money when CDs, records, and tapes are sold. Impresarios, people who organize live performances, make their profit through ticket sales.

Concerts help to promote the performers and their music. This helps to sell recordings, which provides profit for the record companies, musicians, and writers. Skilled technicians and managers are essential for the success of a concert, which also needs to be organized, advertised, and administered. Concerts can take place anywhere from arts centers such as the Lincoln Center in New York City to sporting arenas such as Wembley Stadium in London.

Most of the world's big cities have annual festivals of classical, opera, rock, jazz, folk, or world music. These festivals can be sponsored by private or commercial donations. Investing in live performances is becoming a very important part of the music industry.

△ Movie sound tracks and songs are a major part of the music industry. The Indian film industry, based in Bombay and generally known as Bollywood, produces hundreds of musicals a year.

△ The Bregenz Festival in Austria features large-scale opera productions, such as *Fidelio*, on a floating stage. Over recent years, opera has become hugely popular, with lavish performances and huge audiences.

◁ Writing music for the movies and television brings the work of a composer such as Michael Nyman to the attention of a very wide audience.

Recording and Broadcasting

△ Thomas Edison originally intended his phonograph, an early version of the record player, to be used as an office dictating machine.

∇ Radio tubes, which made radio sound a commercial possibility, were developed from electric lightbulbs. They converted radio waves into electric current.

The first sound recording was made in 1877 by the inventor Thomas Edison. His machine, called a phonograph, stored sound on a cylinder covered with tin foil. Ten years later, Emile Berliner made a breakthrough with the invention of the gramophone, which recorded and played back sound on shellac disks. These not only sounded better but also lasted longer than cylinders.

In the 1880s, the inventors Heinrich Hertz and Guglielmo Marconi learned how to control radio waves. However, it was not until the development of the thermionic tube in 1906 that radio broadcasting became a reality. By the 1920s, most countries had their own radio stations, which created a huge new audience for performers and composers.

In 1948, long-playing (LP) vinyl records appeared. These could store much more sound than the old shellac disks and the quality was better. Since the 1980s, digital technology has revolutionized sound-recording. Compact discs (CDs), mini disks, and digital audio tapes (DAT) have replaced vinyl.

△ In a recording session, the performer plays in a soundproof studio. The music is usually recorded in separate "takes" by the recording engineer.

Digital compact cassette

▷ Over the last hundred years, recording quality has improved enormously from the scratchy sound of the old 78s to the crystal clear quality of compact discs. Audio tapes recorded digitally (DAT) are also of a higher quality.

Mini disk

Digital audio tape

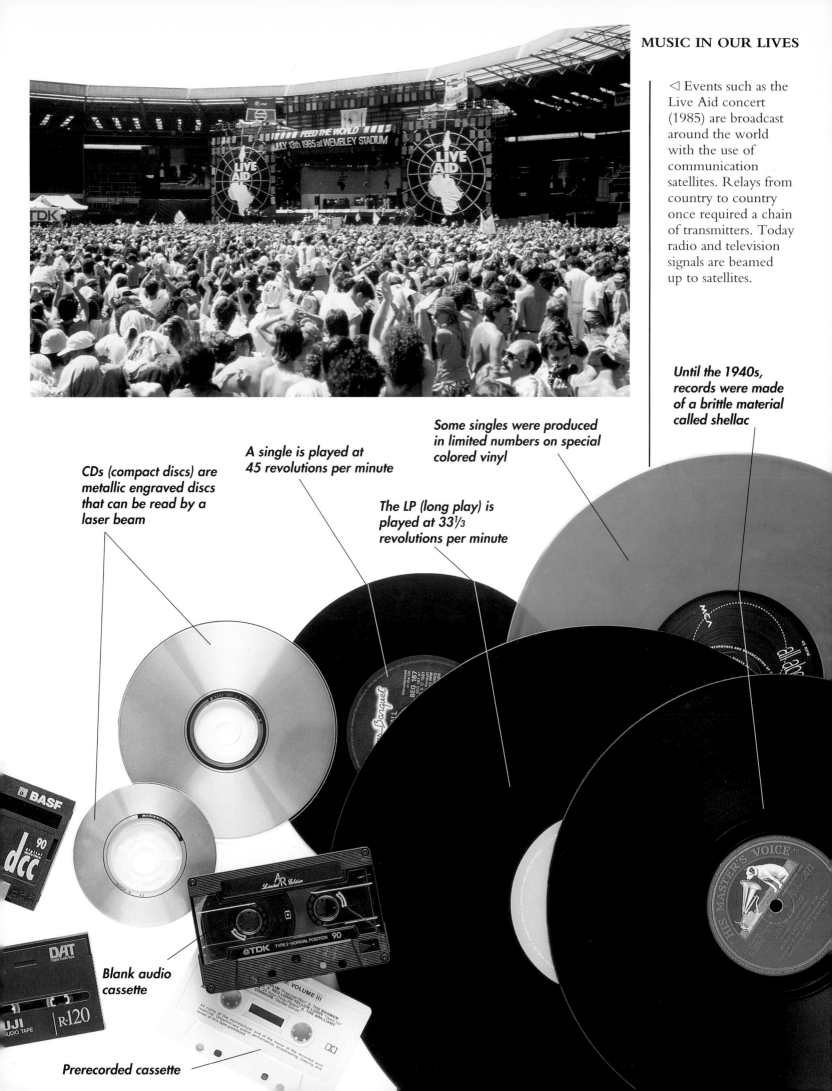

◁ Events such as the Live Aid concert (1985) are broadcast around the world with the use of communication satellites. Relays from country to country once required a chain of transmitters. Today radio and television signals are beamed up to satellites.

Until the 1940s, records were made of a brittle material called shellac

Some singles were produced in limited numbers on special colored vinyl

A single is played at 45 revolutions per minute

CDs (compact discs) are metallic engraved discs that can be read by a laser beam

The LP (long play) is played at 33⅓ revolutions per minute

Blank audio cassette

Prerecorded cassette

Buildings for Music

Churches were among the first public buildings in which music could be heard by large numbers of people. The first theater to be built with the purpose of performing opera—nonreligious music—was opened in Venice, Italy, in 1637. Before this time, opera had only been seen in the palaces and courts of Europe. The idea caught on—twelve more opera houses were built in Venice by the end of the 1600s!

Small public concert halls for the paying public began to open during the 1700s. These became grander and larger in the 1800s to accommodate the growing audiences and orchestras of the day. Today, modern concert halls are built to adapt to all kinds of music including jazz, classical, and pop.

△ J. S. Bach worked for over 25 years at the church of St. Thomas in Leipzig, Germany. His works took into account the building's acoustics.

BUILDINGS ON FIRE!

The opera house in Covent Garden, London, burned to the ground in 1856. Fire had previously destroyed it in 1808. Fire was a constant hazard in theaters until the late 1800s, and music lovers would go to shows or concerts at their own risk. There were over a thousand major fires in European theaters between 1700 and 1800—the average length of time a theater stood before being gutted by fire was just 18 years! The number of fires decreased when electric lighting replaced gas lamps.

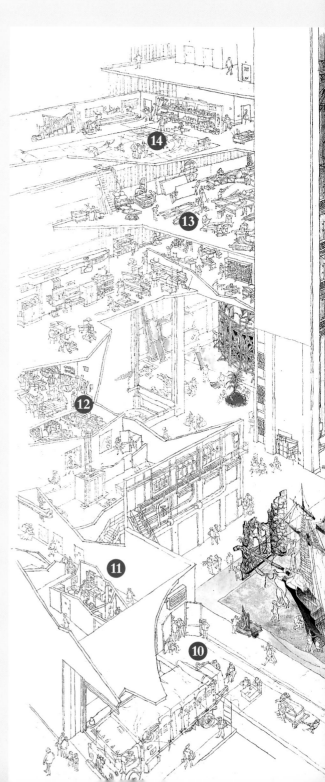

The Metropolitan Opera House in New York as part of the Lincoln Center for the Performing Arts opened in 1966. It is designed in the traditional horseshoe shape that dates back to some of the earliest opera houses built in Venice. You can see: **1** the auditorium, which seats 3,800 people; **2** the orchestra pit; **3** the main stage; **4** the stage manager's desk; **5** and **6** scenery ready to be moved onto the main stage; **7** electrically controlled fly system for hanging backdrops to the main stage; **8** catwalks giving access to stage lighting; **9** strip lights extending across the main stage; **10** the loading bay; **11** dressing rooms; **12** the wardrobe; **13** the carpenters' work area; **14** the paint shop.

Buildings for music come in all shapes and sizes, from small concert rooms suitable for chamber music to huge opera houses.

△ The Opéra in Paris, France, opened in 1875. Built in the grandest style, it can seat over 2,000 people.

△ The shell-shaped roof of the Sydney Opera House is one of the world's best-known landmarks.

△ The Albert Hall in London, houses the famous Prom concerts every summer.

△ The opera house in Manaus, Brazil, stands deep in the rain forest. It was opened in 1896.

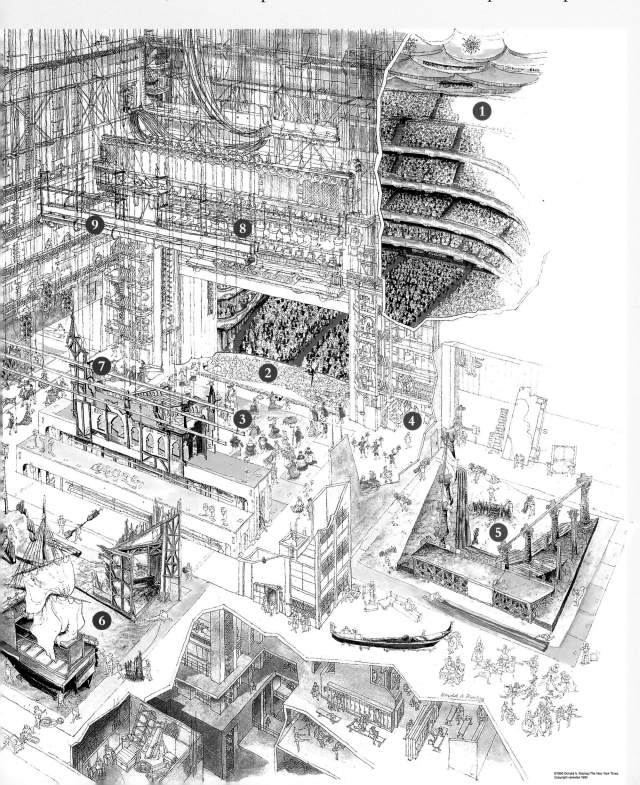

The Great Composers

△ *Title page from one of Bach's cantatas*

ADAMS, JOHN
(b. 1947) American, born in Massachusetts, he studied at Harvard University and taught at the San Francisco Conservatory. His compositions, mainly in the minimalist style, include works for strings and full orchestra, as well as the three-act opera *Nixon in China*.

BACH, JOHANN SEBASTIAN (1685–1750)
German, born in Eisenach. Bach is the best-known member of a remarkable family of musicians. He was orphaned young and brought up by his elder brother, a church organist. He worked as a musician at the courts of Weimar and Köthen before becoming choirmaster of the St. Thomas Church and School in Leipzig. Here he remained for nearly 30 years, producing a vast amount of music, including religious pieces, such as the *St. Matthew Passion*, and music for choir, organ, orchestra, and keyboard instruments. He married twice and had twenty children. Four of his sons became well-known musicians and composers.

BARTÓK, BÉLA (1881–1945)
Hungarian, born in Sinnicolau Mare. He was taught to play the piano by his mother before studying in Bratislava. He was a gifted pianist, and wrote many piano works to play himself. Bartók took a particular interest in Hungarian folk music, and this influenced many of his compositions. In 1940 he moved to the U.S.A. where he spent five busy but unhappy years before dying in poverty.

△ *Ludwig van Beethoven*

BEETHOVEN, LUDWIG VAN (1770–1827)
German, born in Bonn. Beethoven first studied music with his father, a singer at the court of the Elector of Cologne, and later with Haydn, and he soon became famous as the greatest pianist of his time. Although he was a brilliant composer, he never found composing easy. At the age of 32 he began to go deaf, but he continued to compose, producing the *Eroica* symphony in 1804 and the opera *Fidelio* the following year. Remarkably he wrote some of his best works after he had become completely deaf at the age of 50. Beethoven spent most of his adult life in Vienna, supported by a number of aristocratic patrons. Before his death, his fame had spread throughout Europe.

BERG, ALBAN (1885–1935)
Austrian, born in Vienna. He studied with Schoenberg, who had a major influence on his music. One of Berg's best-known works, the opera *Lulu*, was still unfinished at his death.

▷ *Hector Berlioz*

BERLIOZ, HECTOR (1803–1869)
French, born near Grenoble. The son of a doctor, Berlioz studied medicine before taking up music as a career. His music was influenced by the plays of Shakespeare, the Romantic poets, and Beethoven's symphonies. He never achieved acclaim in France and had to make his living as a music critic.

BERNSTEIN, LEONARD (1918–1990)
American, born in Massachusetts. Equally gifted as a conductor, composer, and pianist, Bernstein conducted the New York Philharmonic Orchestra from 1958 to 1969. His works span both popular and classical music. They include three symphonies, as well as successful Broadway musicals—notably the ever-popular *West Side Story*.

BIZET, GEORGES (1838–1875)
French, born in Paris. Bizet entered the Paris Conservatory at nine. He wrote his first symphony in 1855, although it was not performed until 1935. He wrote several unsuccessful operas, then completed his masterpiece, *Carmen*, just before his early death from heart disease.

BOULEZ, PIERRE (b. 1925)
French, born in Montbrison. He studied with Messiaen at the Paris Conservatory. He became one of the leading avant-garde composers of the 1950s. Boulez is also well known as a conductor.

BRAHMS, JOHANNES (1833–1897) German, born in Hamburg. Brahms was the son of a poor double-bass player. When young, he played the piano in inns and dance halls to pay for his musical tuition. Brahms produced a large body of music in most fields except opera, but he is best known for his symphonies and concertos.

BRITTEN, BENJAMIN (1913–1976) English, born in Lowestoft. Britten began composing at the age of five. His first opera *Peter Grimes*, was produced in 1945. Britten wrote several pieces for young people including *The Young Person's Guide to the Orchestra*.

△ *Johannes Brahms*

BYRD, WILLIAM (1543–1623) English, probably born in Lincoln. He was a pupil of Tallis and in 1572 became organist at the Chapel Royal, London. In 1575, Queen Elizabeth I granted Byrd and Tallis a special license to print music. For 21 years only they were allowed to print music in England. Byrd, who wrote sacred music, songs, and keyboard music, is often described as "the father of English music."

CAGE, JOHN (1912–1992) Born in Los Angeles. He studied with Schoenberg. Always exploring new ideas, Cage invented the "prepared piano"—a piano with objects such as screws and paper placed on the strings to distort the sound. One of his most famous works *4' 33"*, consists of four minutes and 33 seconds of silence. Cage was also an expert on fungi.

CARTER, ELLIOTT (b. 1908) Born in New York City. He studied at Harvard and with Nadia Boulanger in Paris. He has taught music at Columbia and Yale Universities and has written symphonies, concertos, ballets, and chamber music.

CHOPIN, FRÉDÉRIC (1810–1849) Polish, born near Warsaw. Chopin was nine when he first played the piano in public. By the age of 16 he had composed several piano works. He moved to Paris in 1831 and quickly became famous as a teacher and composer. Chopin was also known for his good looks. He fell in love with the French female novelist George Sand, who nursed him when he became ill with tuberculosis. They parted in 1848, and he died the following year after touring Great Britain.

COPLAND, AARON (1900–1990) Born in Brooklyn, New York. The young Copland studied in France with the influential teacher Nadia Boulanger. His most famous works are his ballets, such as *Appalachian Spring*, which draw on traditional American music. He also composed operas, symphonies, and movie scores.

COUPERIN, FRANÇOIS (1668–1733) French, born in Paris. Couperin was born into a musical family. His father was organist at the church of St. Gervais, Paris, as were nine other Couperins including François himself. Couperin became organist and harpsichordist to King Louis XIV. His work had an influence on Bach.

DEBUSSY, CLAUDE (1862–1918) French, born in St. Germain-en-Laye, near Paris. His early work was influenced by Wagner, and also by Javanese *gamelan* music. Later compositions have been described as the musical equivalent of Impressionist paintings—pictures in sound. As well as many works for orchestra, such as *La Mer*, Debussy wrote piano music, several ballets, and the opera *Pelléas et Mélisande*.

▽ *Aaron Copland*

DELIUS, FREDERICK
(1862–1934) English, born in Bradford. Delius went to Europe to study music in Leipzig and became friendly with Grieg. From 1890 he lived in France, where he wrote orchestral music and operas. Although he went blind in 1924, he continued to compose until his death.

△ *Frederick Delius*

DESPREZ, JOSQUIN
(1440–1521) French, born in Beaurevoir, Picardy. Desprez (or Josquin as he was often called) was one of the greatest Renaissance composers. He traveled in Italy as a young man and worked for Cardinal Sforza and the Duke of Ferrara. Later he went to live in France. His works, which include masses and motets, were forgotten after his death but rediscovered in the 1700s.

DVOŘÁK, ANTONIN
(1841–1904) Czech, born near Prague. Dvořák's father was a butcher, and Dvořák was a butcher's boy before studying music and the viola at the Prague Organ School. He worked as an orchestra musician, then Brahms helped him to concentrate on composing. Along with Janácek he helped to develop

Czech music. In 1892, however, he went to the U.S.A., and out of homesickness wrote his most famous symphony *From the New World*. He returned to Prague in 1895.

ELGAR, EDWARD
(1857–1934) English, born near Worcester. Elgar was the son of an organist and music dealer. He was mainly self-taught and worked locally as a violinist, organist, teacher, and conductor. His *Enigma Variations* brought success as a composer when he was 42, and in 1901 his *Pomp and Circumstance March no. 1* became a popular piece. Elgar was one of the first composers to make gramophone recordings, but he wrote little after his wife's death in 1920.

FAURÉ, GABRIEL
(1845–1924) French, born in Pamiers. Fauré trained as a pianist and organist under Saint-Saëns, and for much of his life worked as a church musician. In 1905 he became director of the Paris Conservatory, where his pupils included Ravel. Fauré is best known for his songs and his *Requiem*, but also wrote

chamber music and operas. He was troubled by deafness for the last 20 years of his life.

GERSHWIN, GEORGE
(1898–1937) Born in New York City. Gershwin, a talented songwriter, first became famous for his Broadway musicals. Most had lyrics by his brother, Ira. In 1924 his *Rhapsody in Blue* for piano and jazz band brought him success as a serious

△ *George Gershwin*

composer. This was followed by the popular "folk opera" *Porgy and Bess*.

GLASS, PHILIP (b. 1937)
Born in Baltimore. The son of a music shop owner, Glass studied at New York's Juillard School and in Paris. He also worked with the Indian *sitar* musician, Ravi Shankar. Glass became famous with his 1976 minimalist-style opera *Einstein on the Beach*.

GÓRECKI, HENRYK
(b. 1933) Polish, born near Katowice. Górecki studied at the Katowice Conservatory and with Messiaen in Paris. His works are strongly influenced by Polish religious music. Górecki was virtually unknown outside Poland until the 1992 recording of his *Symphony no. 3* achieved worldwide success, selling over a million copies.

◁ *A plaque to mark the birthplace of Edvard Grieg in Bergen, Norway*

△ *Hildegard of Bingen*

GRIEG, EDVARD (1843–1907)
Norwegian, born in Bergen. Grieg was taught by his mother, a pianist, before going on to study at the Leipzig Conservatory. He became very interested in the traditions of Norwegian folk music. His best-known work is his incidental music for *Peer Gynt*, a play by Henrik Ibsen.

HANDEL, GEORGE FRIDERIC (1685–1759)
German-English, born in Halle. The son of a barber-surgeon, Handel became organist of Halle cathedral while still studying law. He was a musician in an opera orchestra, then spent four years in Italy, where he wrote several operas. He then worked for the Elector of Hanover, who later became George I of England. After several visits to England in the early 1700s, Handel moved there permanently, working in the courts of Queen Anne and King George I. He was a prolific composer, writing *Messiah* (with its famous "Hallelujah Chorus"), *Saul*, orchestral pieces, such as his *Water Music* and *Music for the Royal Fireworks,* and over 40 operas. He died after fainting during a performance of *Messiah* and was buried in Westminster Abbey.

HAYDN, JOSEPH (1732–1809)
Austrian, born in Rohrau. Haydn, the son of a wheelwright, was a choirboy at St. Stephen's Cathedral, Vienna. For much of his career he was musical director to the Esterhazys, one of the most powerful families in Hungary. In the 1780s, Haydn twice visited England, where his music was very popular, and was made a doctor of music at Oxford University. He taught Beethoven and was friends with Mozart. He wrote a huge amount of music of all kinds, including 18 operas and 84 string quartets. However, he is best known for his work in developing the symphony as a musical form. He wrote 104 symphonies, and has been called the "father of the symphony."

HILDEGARD OF BINGEN (1098–1179)
German, born in Bemersheim. Hildegard, an abbess, was one of the most famous and remarkable women of her day. She was a gifted composer of sacred music and also a poet, naturalist, and mystic.

HOLST, GUSTAV (1874–1934)
English, born in Cheltenham. Holst studied at the Royal College of Music in London. He worked as a trombonist and became director of music at St. Paul's Girls' School, London. He had a deep interest in English folk songs. His most famous composition is the orchestral suite *The Planets*.

KODÁLY, ZOLTÁN (1882–1967)
Hungarian, born in Kecskemét. Kodály studied at the Liszt Academy of Music and later taught composition there. With Béla Bartók, who was a life-long friend, he began collecting Hungarian folk songs. After Bartók's death in 1945, Kodály was celebrated as Hungary's greatest living composer. Many of his choral works were written for children.

LISZT, FRANZ (1811–1886)
Hungarian, born in Raiding. Liszt, a brilliant pianist and a great showman, first performed in public aged nine. Until 1847 he traveled throughout Europe, giving the concerts that made him famous. Later he became music director at the court of Weimar in Germany. Liszt's works for the piano include his *20 Hungarian Rhapsodies,* and some of his piano compositions rank among the most difficult ever written. At the end of his life he lived in Rome and became deeply religious. One of his daughters, Cosima, married the composer Wagner.

MACHAUT, GUILLAUME DE (c. 1300–1377)
French, born in Rheims. Machaut was a priest and poet who worked at the courts of John of Luxemburg, the Duchess of Normandy, and John, Duke of Berry. His works include both sacred music and songs, many of which are settings for his own poems.

▷ *Franz Liszt*

MAHLER, GUSTAV (1860–1911)
Austrian, born in Kališt, now in the Czech Republic. Mahler studied composition and conducting at the Vienna Conservatory. He held important conducting posts in several European opera houses, such as Budapest, Hamburg, and Vienna. Generally, he used to conduct in the winter and then retreat to the mountains of southern Austria during the summer to compose. He is best known as a composer of symphonies and songs. After 1907 he became conductor of the New York Metropolitan Opera, and then of the New York Philharmonic Orchestra. He returned to Vienna in 1911 because of ill health, and died of pneumonia aged 49.

MENDELSSOHN, FELIX (1809–1847)
German, born in Hamburg. Mendelssohn came from a rich and cultured banking family. He was a gifted pianist as well as a composer; he formed an orchestra when he was 12, and he wrote many works while still in his teens. A journey in 1829 to Scotland inspired his *Hebrides Overture*. His beloved sister, Fanny, was also a composer; after her death, he suffered a series of strokes and died when only 38 years old.

MONTEVERDI, CLAUDIO (1567–1643)
Italian, born in Cremona. Monteverdi studied the violin and composition at Cremona cathedral and became a court musician to the Duke of Mantua. After the Duke's death he was appointed music director of St. Mark's Cathedral, Venice, and became a priest at the age of 65. One of the most inventive of all composers, he helped to develop opera as a musical form. However, only three of his operas survive complete, including *L'incoronazione di Poppea*. He also wrote sacred music and songs.

MOZART, WOLFGANG AMADEUS (1756–1791)
Austrian, born in Salzburg. Mozart was the son of the violinist and composer Leopold Mozart. He was a musical prodigy who was already composing at the age of five, and played the violin for the empress of Austria at six. During his childhood, he and his sister toured Europe giving concerts at many royal courts. In adult life, Mozart was less successful. He worked for the Archbishop of Salzburg but often quarreled with his employer and eventually moved to Vienna. Here he worked as a freelance music teacher, musician, and composer, and he married the singer Constanze Weber. During his short life he composed a huge amount of music: operas, masses, oratorios, nearly 50 symphonies, concertos, and chamber music. In spite of the success of his operas—such as *The Marriage of Figaro, Don Giovanni, Così Fan Tutte,* and *The Magic Flute*—he struggled to make a living and was often in debt. He died from a mysterious illness, possibly typhus, at the age of 35. It has been suggested that he was poisoned by a jealous rival composer, Antonio Salieri, but this is almost certainly untrue.

△ *Mozart's house*

MUSSORGSKY, MODEST (1839–1881)
Russian, born in St. Petersburg. Mussorgsky intended to be a soldier but nervous problems made him resign his army commission. He then concentrated on composing, influenced by Rimsky-Korsakov. Mussorgsky's finest compositions are his operas, which include *Boris Godunov*, but much of his work remained unfinished because of his lifelong habit of heavy drinking. This also resulted in his early death.

PROKOFIEV, SERGEY (1891–1953)
Russian, born in Sontsovska, Ukraine. Encouraged by his mother, a gifted pianist, Prokofiev studied at the St. Petersburg Conservatory, where his teachers included Rimsky-Korsakov. He had a reputation as an ultra-modernist rebel.

△ *Modest Mussorgsky, who died aged only 42*

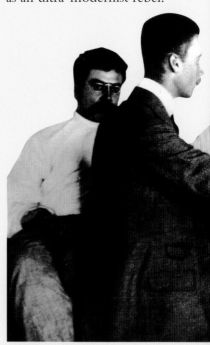

△ *Sergey Prokofiev at the piano*

was written for a competition while he was still a student. He later became the most successful opera composer of his time, and his works are still enormously popular. They include *La Bohème, Madame Butterfly,* and *Turandot.*

PURCELL, HENRY (1659–1695)
English, born in London. Purcell's father was a court musician, and Purcell was a chorister of the Chapel Royal and an organist at Westminster Abbey. He then held a series of court appointments under Charles II, James II, and William III. His varied musical output is celebrated for its sparkling originality. It includes sacred music, songs, instrumental music, and music for stage plays. His brother Daniel was also a composer.

RACHMANINOV, SERGEY (1873–1943)
Russian, born in Nizhniy Novgorod. Rachmaninov studied piano and composition at the Moscow Conservatory and toured Europe as a pianist, becoming famous for his great virtuoso gifts. In 1917 he left Russia and moved to the U.S.A. He is best known for his piano concertos.

RAVEL, MAURICE (1875–1937)
French, born near St. Jean de Luz. A gifted pianist, Ravel studied at the Paris Conservatory and was influenced by Satie, as well as by Eastern music, folk music, and jazz. His delicately balanced music is often compared with that of Debussy. He wrote operas, ballets (such as *Bolero*), and piano music.

△ *Henry Purcell as choirboy*

RIMSKY-KORSAKOV, NIKOLAI (1844–1908)
Russian, born in Tikhvin. Rimsky-Korsakov was a naval officer before becoming a composer, and wrote his first symphony while still in the navy. He then became a professor at the St. Petersburg Conservatory. He wrote 16 operas, the orchestral suite *Scheherazade,* chamber music, and songs. One of his best-loved pieces is *The Flight of the Bumble Bee* from the opera *The Legend of the Czar Sultan.*

RODRIGO, JOAQÚIN (b. 1902)
Spanish, born in Sagunto. Spain's leading composer of the 1900s, Rodrigo went blind at the age of three. He studied in Valencia, then in Paris in 1927. He became famous with his *Concierto de Aranjuez,* in which guitar and orchestra powerfully evoke the landscape of Spain. He later became professor of musical history at Madrid University.

ROSSINI, GIOACHINO (1792–1868)
Italian, born in Pesaro. Rossini's father was a horn player and his mother a singer. He sang in opera as a child and later became director of opera theaters in Naples and Paris. He wrote 36 operas in 19 years, including *The Barber of Seville*—a failure at first but soon hailed as a masterpiece. Later he stopped composing and wrote no more operas during the last 40 years of his life.

SAINT-SAËNS, CAMILLE (1835–1921)
French, born in Paris. As a very young child, Saint-Saëns showed exceptional gifts as pianist. He studied at the Paris

△ *Camille Saint-Saëns*

Conservatory and wrote his first symphony at 17. He was soon considered one of the rebels of French music. He taught music, as well as writing several operas, symphonies (the *Organ Symphony* is the most famous), and pieces for piano and orchestra. His best-known piece, *Carnival of Animals,* was originally written as a joke.

He left Russia in 1918 and lived in England, France, Japan, and the U.S.A., but returned to the Soviet Union in 1934. He lived in Moscow for the rest of his life, dying on the same day as the Soviet dictator Joseph Stalin.

PUCCINI, GIACOMO (1858–1924)
Italian, born in Lucca. Puccini came from a family of professional musicians and worked as a church organist from the age of 14. Later he studied composition at the Milan Conservatory. His first opera

SATIE, ERIK
(1866–1925) French, born in Honfleur. Both of Satie's parents were composers, and he studied at the Paris Conservatory. He is best known for his witty piano pieces and ballets.

SCHOENBERG, ARNOLD (1874–1951)
Austro-Hungarian, born in Vienna. Schoenberg was mainly self-taught. He was helped by the composer Zemlinski, whose sister he married. Schoenberg developed the "12-note" method of composing, which had an important influence on modern music.

SCHUBERT, FRANZ
(1797–1828) Austrian, born in Vienna. The son of a schoolmaster, Schubert learned several instruments as a child and went to Vienna's Royal Chapel choir school. Schubert was a great admirer of Beethoven and often visited the same coffeehouse, but was too shy to introduce himself. In spite of his early death, he produced a large amount of music. He wrote symphonies and chamber music, such as the *Trout Quintet*, but during his lifetime he was best known for his numerous songs.

SCHUMANN, ROBERT
(1810–1856) German, born in Zwickau. The son of a bookseller, Schumann studied law before taking piano lessons with Frederick Wieck, his future father-in-law. He composed symphonies, chamber music, and over 250 songs. He suffered from mental depression and in 1854 entered an asylum, where he died.

SHOSTAKOVICH, DMITRI (1906–1975)
Russian, born in St. Petersburg. Shostakovich studied with his mother, a

△ *Erik Satie*

professional pianist, and then at the Petrograd Conservatory. His *Symphony no. 1* made him famous at the age of 21. After his opera *Lady Macbeth of Mtzensk* was violently criticized in the Soviet press, he concentrated on composing orchestral pieces, concertos, and chamber music. During the appalling siege of Leningrad (St. Petersburg) by the Germans during World War II, he wrote the *7th* or *Leningrad Symphony*, seen at the time as a symbol of freedom.

SIBELIUS, JEAN
(1865–1957) Finnish, born in Hämeenlinna. The son of a surgeon, Sibelius studied law before entering the Helsinki Conservatory. His works, based on Finnish mythology, soon made him famous. He wrote symphonies, symphonic poems (including *Finlandia*), and chamber music. But he became dissatisfied with his work and stopped composing in 1929.

STOCKHAUSEN, KARLHEINZ
(b. 1928) German, born near Cologne. After living through the traumatic years of World War II, in which he lost both his parents, Stockhausen studied in Cologne and Paris. He became famous for his challenging modern music in the 1950s, and his electronic music has influenced both classical composers and rock musicians.

STRAUSS, JOHANN (1825–1899)
Austrian, born in Vienna. Strauss, called "the younger," was the son of composer and conductor Johann Strauss ("the elder") who developed the Viennese waltz. Strauss "the younger" formed his own orchestra and wrote many famous waltzes, such as *The Blue Danube*. He also wrote 16 operettas.

STRAUSS, RICHARD
(1864–1949) German, born in Munich. Richard Strauss was taught music by his father, first horn player in the Munich court opera. He started composing at six and had several works performed before he was 20. He went on to become a leading opera conductor, working in many of the world's great opera houses. As well as operas, he wrote symphonic poems and songs, including the great *Four Last Songs*.

STRAVINSKY, IGOR
(1882–1971) Russian, born near St. Petersburg. The son of an opera singer, Stravinsky was influenced by Debussy. He is best known for his ballets, such as *The Firebird* and *The Rite of Spring*, which he wrote for the Ballets Russes, the exciting Russian ballet company of the early 1900s. He also wrote operas, and orchestral and choral music. He left Russia in 1914 and lived in Switzerland and France before settling in the U.S.A. in 1939.

TALLIS, THOMAS
(1505–1585) English, probably born in London. From 1540, Tallis worked for the English royal household as a singer and organist. He wrote a large amount of church music, as well as keyboard music.

TCHAIKOVSKY, PYOTR ILYICH (1840–1893)
Russian, born in Kamsko-Votkinsk. Tchaikovsky gave up his job in the civil service to study music at the St. Petersburg Conservatory. His music quickly became popular and he was the outstanding Russian composer of his time. His private life was less happy and, though he is said to have died of cholera, he may have committed suicide. He wrote 11 operas and six symphonies, but is perhaps best known for his three ballets,

Swan Lake, The Sleeping Beauty, and *The Nutcracker.*

TIPPETT, MICHAEL
(b. 1905) English, born in London. Having played the piano since the age of five, Tippett studied at the Royal College of Music, London. His 1941 oratorio *A Child of Our Time* made his name as a composer. During World War II he was imprisoned for three months as a conscientious objector. He has written operas, including *King Priam,* symphonies, and numerous choral works.

VAUGHAN WILLIAMS, RALPH (1872–1958)
English, born in Down Ampney. After studying at the Royal College of Music, London, Vaughan Williams was later taught by Ravel. He was much influenced by English folk songs. As well as composing symphonies, operas, and ballets, he was a conductor and taught at the Royal College of Music.

VERDI, GIUSEPPE
(1813–1901) Italian, born in Roncole. Verdi's father was a village innkeeper. He studied

Chiesetta di Roncole

Casa ove nacque G. Verdi a Roncole

NATO IL 10 OTTOBRE 1813

MORTO IL 27 GENNAIO 1901

PROPRIETÀ RISERVATA   Stab. F. Gollini-Milano

△ *A postcard showing Giuseppe Verdi and his birthplace*

music with the organist of Bussetto cathedral and in Milan. He then became music master in Bussetto and began writing operas. Verdi went on to become the most successful opera composer of his generation. The most famous of his 27 operas are *Rigoletto, La Traviata, Aida,* and *Otello.*

VIVALDI, ANTONIO
(1678–1741) Italian, born in Venice. The son of a professional violinist, Vivaldi trained as a priest but soon became famous as a composer. In 1740 he moved to Vienna, hoping to make a success there, but died a year later in poverty. After his death his work was forgotten until his concertos—particularly *The Four Seasons*—became popular in the 1800s.

WAGNER, RICHARD
(1813–1883) German, born in Leipzig. Wagner became interested in opera at an early age. After studying at Leipzig he held a series of positions in

◁ *Dmitri Shostakovich*

German opera houses and then went to Paris, where he worked on his own opera *The Flying Dutchman*. He returned to Germany as music director of the court of Dresden, but had to leave because of his revolutionary activities. He went to Zurich in Switzerland and began work on a set of four operas called *Der Ring des Nibelungen*. This project took 25 years. By 1865 Wagner was in debt, but was saved by the support of King Ludwig II of Bavaria, who invited him to Munich. Ludwig then provided funds for Wagner to build his own opera house at Bayreuth, and he performed his operas here until his death.

WALTON, SIR WILLIAM (1902–1983)
English, born in Oldham. Walton was a chorister at Oxford. His first major work was

Façade, a musical setting for poems by Edith Sitwell. He wrote two symphonies, operas, the oratorio *Belshazzar's Feast,* concertos, and chamber music as well as music scores for movies.

▽ *Richard Wagner*

Classical Music

Facts

The oldest song is the *shaduf* chant sung by workers on the Nile River in Egypt.

The biggest grand piano weighed 1.25 tons and was 11.6 feet (3.55m) long.

Romanian pianist Cella Delavrancea gave her last public performance at the age of 103.

A record audience of 800,000 attended a free concert by the New York Philharmonic Orchestra conducted by Zubin Mehta, 1986.

The largest choir consisted of 60,000 people and sang at the end of a concert in Breslau, Germany on August 2, 1937.

The highest price paid at auction for any instrument was £902,000 for a Stradivarius violin in 1990.

In 1991, Placido Domingo was applauded for 1 hour and 20 minutes after a performance of *Otello*. Luciano Pavarotti received 165 curtain calls at a concert in Berlin in 1988.

The shortest opera ever is *The Sands of Time* by Simon Rees and Peter Reynolds, which at one performance lasted a mere 3 minutes and 34 seconds.

The largest and loudest instrument ever built is the Auditorium Organ in Atlantic City. Now only partly functional, it had the volume of 25 brass bands.

The best-selling classical album is *In Concert* recorded by Carreras, Domingo, and Pavarotti. To date it has sold over 5 million copies.

The most spins in a classical ballet is 32 in *Swan Lake*.

The most expensive piano is a Steinway bought for $390,000 in 1980.

Dates

546 B.C. Pythagoras introduces the concept of the musical octave.

250 B.C. First organ invented in Greece.

A.D. 800 Music becomes widely used in monasteries.

1025 Guido d'Arezzo's first writings on music. He introduced the idea of giving each joint and fingertip on the hand the name of a note as a way of aiding musical memory.

1150 Troubadours become popular in Provence, France.

1240 The motet becomes an important form of polyphonic composition.

1364 One of the first large-scale musical works, Guillaume de Machaut's *Messe de Notre Dame*, is performed at the coronation of Charles V of France in Rheims.

1473 The earliest known printed music, the *Collectorium Super Magnificat* by Johannes Gerson, is published in Esslingen, Germany.

c. 1550 The violin takes the form and shape we know today.

1575 English composers Thomas Tallis and William Byrd jointly publish their *Cantiones Sacrae,* a collection of 34 motets, dedicated to Queen Elizabeth I.

c. 1597 The work thought to be the first example of opera, *La Dafne* (or *Dafne)* by Jacopo Peri, is staged privately at the Corsi Palazzo in Florence.

1610 Monteverdi's *Vespers* is published/composed in Venice.

1637 World's first opera house opens in Venice.

1644 Birth of the great violin maker, Antonio Stradivari.

1709 Bartolommeo Cristofori builds the first pianoforte in Florence.

1721 Bach composes his *Brandenberg Concertos*, a set of 6 *concerti grossi*, dedicated to Christian Ludwig, but apparently never played for him.

1722 Bach writes *The Well Tempered Clavier,* a set of preludes and fugues for keyboard in all the major and minor keys, to show off the advantages of the recently introduced system of "equal temperament."

1725 Vivaldi publishes *The Four Seasons*.

1742 Handel's oratorio *Messiah* premiered in Dublin.

1755 Haydn writes his first quartets.

1761 Publication of Mozart's *Minuet* and *Trio in G*. He was four years old.

1786 First performance of Mozart's *The Marriage of Figaro*.

1798 Haydn's oratorio *The Creation* first performed in Austria.

1787 Mozart wrote the opera *Don Giovanni*.

1794 Haydn completed his *London Symphonies*.

1795 At the age of 13, the Italian violinist Niccolò Paganini makes his first tour.

1815 As well as various other compositions, Schubert writes about 144 songs in this year. Maelzel patents the clockwork metronome.

1824 First performance of Beethoven's *Symphony no. 9*.

1835 Tuba invented in Germany.

1846 Adolphe Sax invents the saxophone.

1851 First performance of Verdi's opera *Rigoletto*, in Venice.

1862 Köchel's catalog of Mozart's works first published.

1871 Verdi's *Aida* first performed not in Italy, but in Cairo. The librettist Gilbert and the composer Sullivan meet and embark on a long collaboration.

1873 Sir George Grove begins compiling his *Dictionary of Music and Musicians*.

1875 First performance of Bizet's opera *Carmen*.

1876 First performance of Wagner's *Ring* operas in Bayreuth.

1877 The phonograph is invented by Edison.

1885 Gilbert and Sullivan finish *The Mikado*.

1887 First performance of Verdi's opera *Otello* in Milan.

1894 The debut of Debussy's *Prélude à l'Apres-midi d'un Faune* causes a scandal because of its supposed "formlessness."

1895 First performance of Puccini's *La Bohème* in Turin.

1903 First performance of Puccini's *Madama Butterfly*, which is a failure. It is revised and presented again in 1904 and is a huge success.

1905 First performance of Debussy's orchestral work, *La Mer*.

1907 First music broadcast.

1910 Stravinsky finishes the music for Diaghilev's ballet *The Firebird*.

1911 First performance of Strauss' opera *Der Rosenkavalier* in Dresden.

1913 Stravinsky's *The Rite of Spring* causes a riot at its premiere in Paris.

1919 First performance of Holst's *The Planets*

c. 1921 Schoenberg devises 12-tone system of composition. Earliest examples of this are the *Suite* for piano and the *5 Piano Pieces*.

1924 First performance of Gershwin's *Rhapsody in Blue*.

1928 First performance of Ravel's *Bolero*, which is originally written as a ballet score.

1931 Walton's dramatic cantata *Belshazzar's Feast* is first performed at Leeds Festival.

1935 First performance of Gershwin's *Porgy and Bess* in Boston.

1936 First performance of Prokofiev's *Peter and the Wolf*.

1937 First performance of Orff's *Carmina Burana*.

c. 1941 First performance of Copland's *Appalachian Spring*.

1946 First performance of Prokofiev's *War and Peace*, in Leningrad.

1949 First performance of Messaien's *Turangalîla Symphony*, which uses unusual instruments such as the ondes martenot.

1954 First performance of Varèse's *Déserts*, the first work to combine musical instruments and prerecorded magnetic tape.

1955 First performance of Boulez's *Le Marteau sans maître*.

1961 First performance of Britten's *War Requiem*.

1984 First performance of *Akhnaten* by Glass, in Stuttgart.

1989 First performance of Tippett's opera *New Year*, in London.

1990 Pavarotti, Domingo, and Carreras sing at the soccer World Cup Finals in Rome.

1992 First performance of Stockhausen's opera *Dienstag aus Licht* in Portugal.

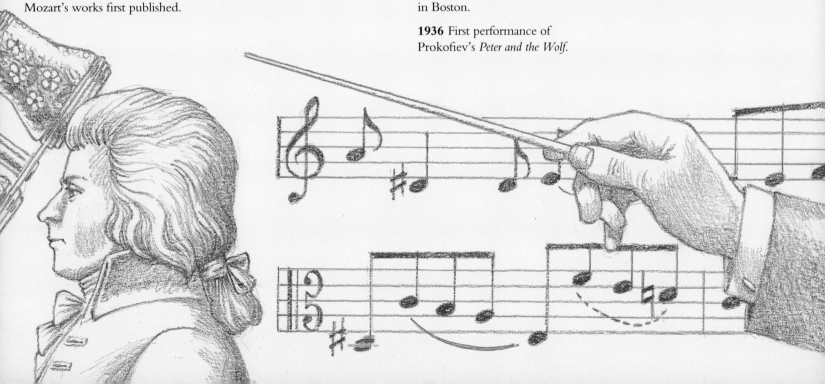

Musicals

Facts

A Chorus Line holds the record for the longest run on Broadway with 6,137 performances.

The longest-running musical of all is the off-Broadway show, *The Fantastiks,* which totaled 14,488 performances.

The longest-running musical in London's West End is *Cats.* It passed *A Chorus Line*'s record on January 29, 1996, making it the longest-running major show on either side of the Atlantic.

Miss Saigon holds the record for the largest advance sales at the box office at $36m before its 1991 opening on Broadway.

In 1978, Columbia Pictures paid $9.8m for the film rights to the musical *Annie.*

26.5 million copies of the *Saturday Night Fever* (1977) sound track were sold up to May 1987, making it the top-selling film sound track.

The sound track of the film *South Pacific* was No.1 in the first UK album charts in 1958.

Classic Stage Musicals

1915 *Very Good, Eddie*—Jerome Kern and Guy Bolton

1924 *Lady, Be Good*—George and Ira Gershwin

1927 *Show Boat*—Jerome Kern and Oscar Hammerstein II

1928 *The Threepenny Opera*—Kurt Weill and Bertolt Brecht

1929 *Mr. Cinders*—Vivian Ellis; *Bitter Sweet*—Noel Coward

1934 *Anything Goes*—Cole Porter

1935 *Porgy and Bess*—George and Ira Gershwin

1937 *Me and My Girl*—Noel Gay, Douglas Furber, and L. Arthur Rose

1940 *Pal Joey*—Richard Rogers and Lorenz Hart

1943 *Oklahoma!*—Richard Rogers and Oscar Hammerstein II

1956 *My Fair Lady*—Fritz Loewe and Alan Jay Lerner

1957 *West Side Story*—Leonard Bernstein and Stephen Sondheim

1960 *Oliver!*—Lionel Bart; *The Fantastiks*—Harvey Schmidt and Tom Jones

1964 *Fiddler on the Roof*—Jerry Beck and Sheldon Harnick

1966 *Cabaret*—John Kander and Fred Ebb

1968 *Hair*—Galt MacDermot, James Rado, and Gerome Rgni

1972 *Jesus Christ, Superstar*—Andrew Lloyd Webber and Tim Rice

1973 *A Little Night Music*—Stephen Sondheim

1975 *A Chorus Line*—Marvin Hamlisch and Edward Kleban

1978 *Evita*—Andrew Lloyd Webber and Tim Rice

1984 *Sunday in the Park with George*—Stephen Sondheim

1985 *Les Misérables*—Claude-Michel Schönberg and Alain Boublil

1986 *The Phantom of the Opera*—Andrew Lloyd Webber and Charles Hart

1993 *Sunset Boulevard*—Andrew Lloyd Webber and Don Black

Classic Musicals Conceived as Movies

1929 *Broadway Melody*—Nacio Herb Brown and Arthur Freed

1933 *42nd Street*—Harry Warren and Al Dubin

1935 *Top Hat*—Irving Berlin

1937 *Shall We Dance?*—George and Ira Gershwin

1939 *The Wizard of Oz*—Harold Arlen and Yip Harburg

1944 *Meet Me in St. Louis*—Hugh Martin and Ralph Blame

1948 *Easter Parade*—Irving Berlin

1951 *An American In Paris*—Nacio Herb Brown and Arthur Freed

1952 *Singin' in the Rain*—Nacio Herb Brown and Arthur Freed

1953 *The Band Wagon*—Arthur Schwartz and Howard Dietz

1954 *A Star is Born*—Harold Arlen and Ira Gershwin

1958 *Gigi*—Fritz Loewe and Alan Jay Lerner; *King Creole*—Jerry Lieber and Mike Stoller

Jazz

Jazz Terms

Bebop A name used to describe the jazz of Charlie Parker and others, but originally meaning "Go, man, go!" in African-American slang.

Combo Abbreviation of combination. A group of musicians.

Dixieland Often used to describe New Orleans jazz, the term may derive from the French word "dix" meaning ten and the $10 bill was printed in New Orleans.

Hip To be aware of new developments in music and fashion; "with it."

Horn Jazz term for any brass or woodwind instrument.

Jam session An informal gathering of musicians playing jazz for their own enjoyment.

Riff A repeated, brief, distinctive musical phrase.

Syncopation One of the key attributes of jazz, it involves accenting normally unstressed beats in a musical bar.

Classic Jazz Recordings

1916 *Scott Joplin*

1923 *The Complete 1923 OKehs*—King Oliver's Jazz Band

1924–1928 *The Bix Beiderbecke Legend*

1925–1927 *The Bessie Smith Story Vol. 3*

1926–1928 *The King of New Orleans Jazz*—Jelly Roll Morton

1927–1946 *At His Very Best*—Duke Ellington

1928 *Louis Armstrong and Earl Hines*

1935–1941 *Ella Fitzgerald Vol. 1*

1936–1940 *Lester Young Memorial Album*—Lester Young and Count Basie

1937–1938 *The Golden Years Vol. 2*—Billie Holiday

1938 *The Carnegie Hall Concert*—Benny Goodman

1946 *Ol' Man Rebop*—Dizzie Gillespie

1946–1947 *Bird Lives*—Charlie Parker; *Sassy Sings*—Sarah Vaughan

1947 *Genius of Modern Music*—Thelonius Monk

1949–1950 *Birth of the Cool*—Miles Davis

1954 *A Night at Birdland*—Art Blakey

1956 *Saxophone Colossus*—Sonny Rollins

1957 *The Hawk Flies High*—Coleman Hawkins

1958 *Somethin' Else*—Cannonball Adderley; *The Sermon*—Jimmy Smith

1959 *Time Out*—Dave Brubeck; *The Shape of Jazz to Come*—Ornette Coleman; *Kind of Blue*—Miles Davis

1960 *My Favorite Things*—John Coltrane

1963 *The Black Saint and the Sinner Lady*—Charles Mingus; *Our Man in Paris* – Dexter Gordon; *Night Train*—Oscar Peterson

1964 *The Sidewinder*—Lee Morgan

1969 *Bitches' Brew*—Miles Davis

1972 *Head Hunter*—Herbie Hancock

1975 *Native Dancer*—Wayne Shorter

1977 *Heavy Weather*—Weather Report

1982 *Bobby McFerrin*

1985 *Song X*—Pat Metheny

1986 *Standard Time*—Wynton Marsalis; *On the Edge of Tomorrow*—Steve Coleman

1991 *The Language of Truth*—Julian Joseph

1992 *To the Eyes of Creation*—Courtney Pine

Rock and Pop

Facts

Between 300,000 and 500,000 people attended the first of the giant pop festivals, the Woodstock Music and Art Fair in Bethel, New York from August 15–17, 1969.

The estimated 3.5 million people who saw Rod Stewart play a free concert in Rio de Janeiro, on New Year's Eve 1988, are thought to be the biggest rock audience ever.

Michael Jackson played to 504,000 people on seven sellout nights at Wembley Stadium, London, in July and August 1988.

The Rolling Stones have won the most gold records for a group—39. Chicago won the most platinum records with 17. Paul McCartney has won 13 platinum discs, the most for any male performer.

Stevie Wonder, with 17 awards, is the top Grammy Award winner.

Elvis Presley's estate was presented with 50 platinum and 60 gold discs, a world record.

Michael Jackson won a record 8 Grammy Awards in 1984.

"Rock Around the Clock," released in 1954 by Bill Haley and his Comets, is estimated to have sold the most copies of any single at 25 million.

Michael Jackson's *Thriller* (1982) is the best-selling album of all time, with worldwide sales of over 47 million copies.

Fleetwood Mac's *Rumours* (1970) has sold 21 million copies, making it the best-selling album by any group.

The best-selling album in the UK is The Beatles' *Sgt. Pepper's Lonely Hearts Club Band* (1967).

The Beatles' "Can't Buy Me Love" (1964) had the greatest advance sales of any single with 2.2 million copies ordered worldwide.

Bat Out of Hell (1979) by Meat Loaf totaled the most weeks on the UK album chart with 471 up to April 1994.

Pink Floyd's *Dark Side of the Moon* (1973) spent a record 741 weeks in the album charts up to the end of 1992.

"My Way" (1969) by Frank Sinatra totaled the most weeks spent on the UK singles chart with 77.

"Tainted Love" (1987) by Soft Cell spent a record 43 weeks in a row on the Billboard Hot 100.

The Beatles hold the record for the most consecutive UK No.1 singles with 11.

The Beatles had a record 20 No.1 singles.

Bryan Adams' "(Everything I Do) I Do for You" (1992) spent a record 16 consecutive weeks at No.1 in the UK singles chart.

Whitney Houston's "I Will Always Love You" (1992) and Boyz II Men's "I'll Make Love to You" (1994) hold the record jointly for the longest stay at No.1 in the singles chart with 14 weeks.

Cliff Richard holds the record for the most UK hit singles, with 115 up to December 1994.

Elvis Presley had a record 149 releases on the Billboard singles chart up to 1990.

The Beatles had a record 15 No.1 albums in the charts. Elvis Presley had the most hit albums with 92.

In 1991, Michael Jackson signed a $890m recording contract with Sony—believed to be the largest music contract in history.

Classic Releases

Singles

1955 "Rock around the Clock"—Bill Haley and the Comets

1956 "Heartbreak Hotel"—Elvis Presley

1958 "All I Have To Do Is Dream"—The Everly Brothers

1959 "It Doesn't Matter Any More"—Buddy Holly

1960 "Three Steps to Heaven"—Eddie Cochran

1963 "I Want to Hold Your Hand"—The Beatles

1964 "Pretty Woman"—Roy Orbison

1965 "Satisfaction"—The Rolling Stones

1966 "River Deep and Mountain High"—Ike and Tina Turner

1967 "All You Need is Love"—The Beatles

1968 "Sitting on the Dock of the Bay"—Otis Redding

1969 "I Heard It Through the Grapevine"—Marvin Gaye

1971 "Hot Love"—T Rex

1972 "School's Out"—Alice Cooper

1975 "Bohemian Rhapsody"—Queen

1976 "Anarchy in the UK"—The Sex Pistols

1979 "Sunday Girl"—Blondie

1981 "Tainted Love"—Soft Cell

1983 "Billie Jean"—Michael Jackson

1984 "Do They Know it's Christmas?"—Band Aid

1985 "Into the Groove"—Madonna

1987 "It's A Sin"—The Pet Shop Boys

1990 "Ice Ice Baby"—Vanilla Ice

1991 "(Everything I Do) I Do For You"—Bryan Adams

1992 "I Will Always Love You"—Whitney Houston

1993 "I'll Do Anything For Love (But I Won't Do That)"—Meat Loaf

1994 "Love Is All Around"—Wet Wet Wet

Albums

1963 *With the Beatles*—The Beatles

1964 *Bringing It All Back Home*—Bob Dylan

1965 *Aftermath*—The Rolling Stones

1966 *Revolver*—The Beatles

1967 *Sgt. Pepper's Lonely Hearts Club Band*—The Beatles

1968 *Electric Ladyland*—Jimi Hendrix

1969 *Tommy*—The Who

1970 *Bridge Over Troubled Water*—Simon and Garfunkel

1971 *Imagine*—John Lennon

1972 *Ziggy Stardust*—David Bowie

1973 *Tubular Bells*—Mike Oldfield

1974 *Queen 2*—Queen

1975 *Blood on the Tracks*—Bob Dylan

1976 *Hotel California*—The Eagles

1977 *Rumours*—Fleetwood Mac

1978 *This Year's Model*—Elvis Costello

1979 *Bat Out of Hell*—Meat Loaf

1980 *Hotter Than July*—Stevie Wonder

1982 *Thriller*—Michael Jackson

1983 *Swordfishtrombones*—Tom Waits

1984 *Born in the USA*—Bruce Springsteen

1985 *Brothers in Arms*—Dire Straits

1986 *Graceland*—Paul Simon

1987 *Tunnel of Love*—Bruce Springsteen

1988 *Naked*—Talking Heads

1989 *New York*—Lou Reed

1990 *Immaculate Collection*—Madonna

1991 *Stars*—Simply Red

1992 *Automatic for the People*—REM

1993 *Home Invasion*—Ice-T

1994 *Park Life*—Blur

1995 *What's the Story, Morning Glory*—Oasis

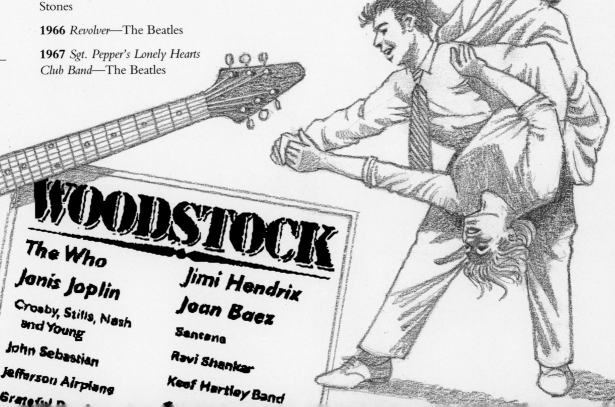

Glossary

Absolute music Instrumental music composed purely as music, without aiming to tell a story or interpret a work of art. The opposite of program music.

Accidental A sign, such as a sharp, flat, or natural, which is used in music notation to alter the pitch of a note. An accidental not only affects the note that follows it, but also any other notes of the same pitch that appear later in the bar. After a barline, the notes return to their normal pitch.

Accompaniment The musical background that supports the main part in a piece of music. For example, a singer might perform songs "with piano accompaniment."

Acoustics The science of sound and how it is produced. *Also,* the characteristics of a building (e.g. shape, size), which affect how sound is heard. For example, a concert hall will be designed to have good acoustics so that the audience will be able to hear clearly and without distortion.

Aerophone A musical instrument that uses vibrating air to produce a sound. Most aerophones are blown by the performer (e.g. flute, trumpet, bagpipe), but some use a mechanical device to make air vibrate (e.g. organ).

Aleatory music A type of music in which some parts of the composition or performance are left to chance. For example, this might mean asking the performer to throw dice to decide which section to play next, interpret a graphic score, or improvise.

Anthem A short piece for choir on a religious theme. An anthem is similar to a motet, but is used in the Protestant, not the Roman Catholic, church and sung in English instead of Latin. *Also,* a hymnlike song that is used for special occasions. For example, the national anthem.

Antiphony The effect created when two groups of musicians, positioned some distance apart, perform alternately so that one group seems to be "answering" the other.

Aria A vocal piece, generally for just one singer, with instrumental accompaniment. Arias are usually found in large compositions such as operas.

▽ *Bagpipes*

Arpeggio A chord in which the notes are played one after the other instead of all at the same time. Sometimes notes are played from top to bottom, but usually from bottom to top.

Arrangement A piece of music that has been adapted so that it can be played by instruments other than those the composer intended. For example, a composition for orchestra might be "arranged" so that it could be played on the piano.

Atonal music Music that has no key. Atonal music treats all twelve notes of the chromatic scale equally.

Ballet A form of entertainment in which performers dance and mime to music. The dancers interpret the music using a variety of movements and expressions to create moods and tell stories.

Bar A small section of a piece of music. Music is split up into bars by vertical lines known as barlines, and each bar contains the number of beats shown in the time signature. A double barline (a thin line followed by a thick one) is used at the end of a piece.

Baroque music Music that was composed during the period from 1600 to 1750. Composers such as Johann Sebastian Bach, Antonio Vivaldi, and George Frideric Handel wrote during this period. Many musical forms became important at this time, including the opera, oratorio, sonata, and dance suite. The term *Baroque* is also used to describe art and architecture.

Beat A unit of time used in music. In each bar, notes are grouped together in beats to make them easier to read. For example, in 3/4 the notes are grouped in three quarter beats. In 6/8 they are grouped in two dotted quarter beats.

Blues A kind of folk music that first became popular in the United States in the 1860s. It was based on spiritual and work songs and is often sad and slow. The blues often uses a 12-bar chord sequence and special "blue notes" (flattened notes) to create its distinctive sound. It has influenced many other types of music, especially jazz.

Cadence The end of a phrase or section of a piece of music. A cadence is generally made up of two chords, played one after the other. Sometimes the chords make the music sound complete and finished (perfect cadence), but sometimes they sound incomplete (imperfect cadence) or unexpected (interrupted cadence).

Cadenza A section in a composition for a solo performer where the accompaniment stops playing and the soloist has the opportunity to show off their technique. Cadenzas are most often found in concertos. In some cases they are written by the composer and in others they are left for the performer to improvise.

Canon A piece made up of different parts that copy one another. Each part uses exactly the same notes, but they start at different times, each new one joining a short time after the last. A simple form of canon is called a round.

Carol   A type of song used to celebrate many different occasions such as religious festivals and the changing of the seasons. Today, the word "carol" is generally used to describe a song or hymn that is sung at Christmastime.

Chamber music   Music performed by a small group of people, rather than by a soloist or an orchestra. For example, a string quartet or a piano trio.

Chord   Any two or more notes that are played at the same time. Chords create harmony in music and make it sound complete.

Chordophone   A musical instrument that produces a sound when a string is made to vibrate, by plucking (e.g. guitar, harp), hitting (e.g. piano), or bowing (e.g. violin, cello).

▷ *A cello (chordophone)*

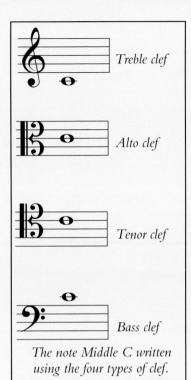

Chorus   A group of singers in a vocal composition. Unlike soloists, the chorus all sing together, either in unison, or in smaller groups with several voices to each part. *Also,* the part of a song that is repeated between verses, sometimes also called the "refrain."

Chromatic scale A musical scale that is made up of 12 notes, each a half step apart. For example, on the piano you can find a chromatic scale by playing from any one note to the next one with the same letter name, using all the black and white keys in between.

Classical music   In the strictest sense, music mainly composed during the period from 1750 to 1830, by composers such as Joseph Haydn, Wolfgang Amadeus Mozart, and Ludwig van Beethoven. During this time, many of the musical forms used today became very important—for example, the symphony, the concerto, and the string quartet. However, in general the word now means music that is more permanent than popular or light music.

Clef   A sign that is placed at the beginning of each line of a piece of music. By looking at the clef it is possible to determine the exact pitch of all the notes on and around the stave. There are four different types of clef—treble, alto, tenor, and bass.

Coda   A final section of a piece, carefully composed to make the music sound as though it has come to an end.

Concerto   A piece for one or more solo instruments and orchestra, usually in three movements. Concertos are popular as showpieces because they give the performer(s) plenty of opportunity to display their virtuosity and technique— particularly in the cadenzas.

Concert pitch Musicians tune instruments to concert pitch so that when they play together they are in tune. It is internationally agreed that at concert pitch the A above

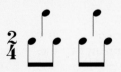

Treble clef

Alto clef

Tenor clef

Bass clef

The note Middle C written using the four types of clef.

middle C has a frequency of 440 hertz. That means it is made up of 440 vibrations per second.

Conductor   The person who directs a group of instrumentalists or singers, such as an orchestra or a choir. Conducting not only involves keeping a steady beat and making sure that everyone plays or sings at the right time, but also interpreting the music. It is the conductor's job to decide on tempo, dynamics, and phrasing, as well as to check that there is a good balance of sound, with no one part sounding too loud or too soft.

△ *A conductor*

Continuo   A kind of accompaniment often used in Baroque music. The continuo part was generally played by a combination of instruments such as cello and harpsichord, with one playing the bass line and the other improvising harmonies around it.

Counterpoint   The combination of two or more independent lines of music. In "contrapuntal" music (music that uses counterpoint), there are often many different melodic lines all playing at the same time—not just one playing the tune and others accompanying it. Similar to polyphony.

Descant   The part sung by the highest voices in a piece of choral music. *Also,* a high counter melody (a melody that is not the main tune), sung by sopranos or trebles in a well-known song such as a hymn.

Duet   A piece for two instruments or voices, either with or without accompaniment.

Duple time   Music that has two beats in each bar for example, 2/4 (below) or 6/8.

Dynamics   The different levels of volume used in music. Dynamic markings tell the performer how loudly or softly to play and when to change from one volume to another. The most commonly used dynamic markings are:
fortissimo (**ff**) = very loud
forte (**f**) = loud
crescendo = get gradually louder
mezzo forte (**mf**) = quite loud
diminuendo = get gradually quieter
piano (**p**) = quiet

mezzo piano (**mp**) = quite quiet
pianissimo (or **pp**) = very quiet

Electrophone   A musical instrument that produces sound electronically, such as a synthesizer.

Encore   A French word that means "again". At the end of

a concert, the audience may shout "Encore!" as a way of asking the performer to play some more, perhaps to repeat something they have already played, or to play something completely different. The piece that is played as a result is also known as an encore.

Fingering   The technique of using the fingers to produce a note from a musical instrument. Small numbers are sometimes printed above or below notes to help musicians determine which fingers to use, especially in music for keyboard instruments such as the piano.

Flat   A sign that lowers the pitch of the note that follows it by a half step. It also affects all other notes of the same pitch that appear later in the same bar. *Also,* a word that describes a musical sound or performance that is lower in pitch than it should be. e.g. "Her singing was flat."

Folk music   Tunes and songs that are passed on from one generation of people to the next, sometimes without ever being written down. Folk songs were generally found among rural dwellers, and spread to cities during the 1700s and 1800s. Some of the

most common types of folk music are children's songs, dance tunes, and songs that are used in rituals and religious ceremonies. Many composers have made use of folk music in their compositions from the Renaissance to Joseph Haydn, Edvard Grieg, Pyotr Tchaikovsky, Ralph Vaughan Williams, and Béla Bartók.

Fret   A strip of wood, metal, or gut that runs across the fingerboard of a stringed instrument such as a guitar, lute, or *sitar*. The violin has no frets. Frets are used to show the player where the fingers need to be placed in order to produce particular notes.

Fugue   A type of contrapuntal piece (see *counterpoint*) in which musical ideas are first played by one part, then imitated by others, with each one joining in a short while after the last.

Fundamental   The name for the lowest harmonic.

Gagaku   A Japanese word meaning "graceful or elegant music," and used to describe an art form involving both music and dancing.

Gamelan   A type of orchestra found in Southeast Asia, particularly on the islands of Java and Bali. Although there are many different kinds of *gamelan,* they all include percussion instruments such as gongs, metallophones, and drums. Some also include flutes and stringed instruments.

Graphic score   A score that uses pictures and symbols instead of ordinary musical notation. The performer creates the music by looking at the score and imagining the sounds, dynamics, and moods the signs represent.

Gregorian chant *see* **plainsong**

Half step   Half a tone. The smallest interval between any two notes on a keyboard.

Harmonics   Each musical sound is made up of lots of different vibrations. For example, when a string vibrates, it not only vibrates as a whole, but also in halves, thirds, quarters, and so on. Each kind of vibration produces a different pitch, known as a harmonic. It is usually only possible to hear the lowest, loudest harmonic (in this case, the sound of the whole string vibrating)—this is called the fundamental.

Harmony   The sounding of different notes at the same time to form chords. The movement from one chord to another is a harmonic progression. With melody and rhythm, harmony is one of the most important elements used in music.

Hymn   A religious song. Hymns have been used for many centuries in the Christian churches.

Idiophone   A musical instrument that produces a sound when it is hit, scraped, or rubbed. In an idiophone, the sound is made by the vibration of the instrument itself (e.g. gong, triangle), not by a separate string, as in a violin (*chordophone*), or skin, as in a drum (*membranophone*).

Improvisation   The process of making up music as you go along, without playing from a musical score or from memory. It is often used in pieces where some of the decisions are left to the performer—for example, in the cadenzas of a concerto, or in compositions that use unusual notation. It is also an important feature of jazz.

Interval   The distance in pitch between any two notes, measured by counting up the notes of the scale from one to the other. The distance from C to G is five notes, C-D-E-F-G. The interval between C and G is called a fifth.

Intonation   The tuning of a musician's performance. If someone has "good intonation," it means that they are in tune, if they have "bad intonation" they are out of tune.

Jazz   A type of music that first appeared in the United States around 1890. It has many influences including the blues, traditional African rhythms, ragtime, work songs, gospel singing, and music that was popular in Europe in the late 1900s.

A jazz band

Jazz often uses syncopated rhythms and improvisation around a melody line or a chord sequence. There are many different kinds, including New Orleans style, Dixieland, swing, bebop, cool, fusion and free-form.

Jongleur   During the Middle Ages, a jongleur was a professional entertainer who traveled from place to place. As well as singing and playing an instrument, a jongleur would probably also have been a skilled acrobat or juggler. Similar to a minstrel.

Kettledrum   Tuned percussion instrument with a single skin stretched over a pot or vessel body. In the orchestra, kettledrums are often known as timpani.

Key   The scale around which a piece of music is based. A piece that mainly uses the notes of the scale of C major, is said to be "in the key of C major." The first note of the scale, which gives it its name, is called the "keynote." *Also,* a lever on an instrument, such as a piano or flute, that is pressed down to produce a note.

Keyboard   The arrangement of levers or keys on an instrument such as a piano or organ.

Key signature   A sign that is written after the clef at the beginning of each line of a piece of music. It is usually made up of one or more sharps or flats, which show the performer which key the music is in, and which notes need to be sharpened or flattened when playing it.

Koto   A Japanese long-necked zither, with 13 silk strings stretched over adjustable bridges.

Ledger/leger lines   Short lines that are added above or below the staff when writing notes that are too high or low to fit on the staff itself.

Legato   An instruction to play smoothly, without pausing between notes.

Libretto   The words of a piece of music such as an opera, oratorio, or cantata.

Lieder   A German word meaning "song." It is generally used to describe a type of vocal composition that was popular with German and Austrian composers during the Romantic period of the 1800s. Lieder are songs for solo voice and piano, with the piano part sometimes acting as an accompaniment to the vocal line, and sometimes as an equal partner.

Madrigal   A kind of vocal composition, generally for several voices without accompaniment. Madrigals were first sung in Italy toward the end of the 1200s, and became especially popular in the 1500s. Unlike motets and anthems, the words in madrigals were not based on religious texts, but on poems about love and country life.

Major scale   One of the most commonly used scales in Western music, the major scale is always made up of the same pattern of intervals. The distance between each pair of notes in the scale is a tone—apart from notes three and four and notes seven and eight, which are both a half step apart. To find the scale of C major on a piano keyboard, simply play from one C to the next, using only the white keys.

Mass   A large composition for choir that is based on the main service of the Roman Catholic church. Sometimes there is also instrumental accompaniment and solo singers.

Melody   A series of notes (of varying pitch) that is played one after the other to form a musical line, or tune. Along with harmony and rhythm, melody is one of the most important elements used in music.

Membranophone   A musical instrument that produces a sound when a stretched "membrane" or skin is made to vibrate. Many kinds of drum are known as membranophones. They are usually struck by the hand or a beater.

Tsuzumi drum

Middle C   The C that is nearest to the middle of the piano keyboard.

MIDI   A word that stands for "Musical Instrument Digital Interface." Most pieces of electronic musical equipment such as keyboards, synthesizers and samplers use MIDI to communicate with one another. Instruments or computers that use MIDI are said to be "MIDI compatible."

Minor scale   A type of scale that has two different forms, the harmonic minor and the melodic minor. As the names suggest, the notes of the harmonic minor scale are mainly used in the harmonies of a piece of music, and the notes of the melodic scale are used in the melody line or tune. The melodic minor scale is unusual, because it uses one set of notes to go up the scale and another to come down again. However, there is one important feature that is common to both types of scale, the third note (or "degree") of any minor scale is a half step lower than in a major scale beginning on the same note. (Here is a picture of part of the G melodic minor scale.)

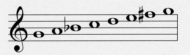

Minstrel   A professional musician and entertainer who lived during the Middle Ages—particularly one who could play at least one sort of musical instrument. Like jongleurs, minstrels sometimes worked with other performers such as troubadours, accompanying their songs on the lute.

Minuet   A type of French dance in triple time. It was originally popular with composers of dance music during the Baroque period. Later, Classical composers such as Wolfgang Amadeus Mozart began to use it too, often as a movement of a work such as a symphony or string quartet.

Modes   One of the scales on which most Western music was based until the end of the 1500s. Modes have traditionally been used in forms of church music such as Gregorian chant, or plainsong, and also in folk music. Two of the modes, the Ionian (the white keys from C to C on a piano) and the Aeolian (the white keys from A to A) were adapted to become the major and minor scales.

Monophony A word meaning "single sound," used to describe music made up of a single melodic line with no accompaniment.

Motet A short choral piece, generally with words based on the Latin texts used in the Roman Catholic church. Motets are often sung unaccompanied. Similar to an anthem.

Movement One of the separate sections found in a composition such as a symphony, string quartet, concerto, or sonata. Pieces often contain several different movements, each one in a slightly different mood or tempo. For example, there are often four movements in a symphony, three in a concerto, and so on.

Natural A sign that is used during a piece of music to cancel a flat or a sharp sign that appears either earlier in the same bar, or in the key signature. Like other accidentals, a natural affects all other notes of the same pitch that follow it in a bar. *Also* the name for a note that is not sharpened or flattened. For example, the note C can also be called C natural.

Notation A way of writing music down. There are many different types of musical notation used around the world, but the Western system of writing notes on the lines and spaces of a staff is one of the most popular.

Note A musical sound, or the sign used to write it down.

Note values
Quarter note A note that lasts for one count. Also called a "crotchet."
Half note A note that lasts for two counts. Also called a "minimo."
Eighth note A note that lasts for half a count. Also called a "quaver."
Whole note A note that lasts for four counts. Also called a "semibreve."
Sixteenth note A note that lasts for a quarter of a count. Also called a "semibreve."

Quarter note

Half note

Eighth note

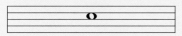
Whole note

Sixteenth note

Octave An interval of eight notes. This is the distance between any note and the note immediately above or below it that shares the same letter name.

Open string A string on an instrument such as a violin that is not "stopped" or pressed down by the fingers.

Opera A dramatic work in which a story is told through singing and acting. Like a play, an opera is performed on a stage (generally in an opera house or theater), with

lighting and special costumes for the cast. An orchestra usually performs an overture at the beginning of the opera, and also accompanies the singers in arias and choruses.

Opus A word meaning work, which is used by composers when keeping records of their compositions. Each piece of music is given an opus number when it is composed or published for the first time, for example "op. 28." When pieces are composed as a group, they usually share opus numbers, for example "op. 101 no. 1," "op. 102 no. 2" and so on.

Oratorio A composition, usually based on a religious story, which is performed by vocal soloists, chorus, and orchestra. The earliest oratorios were acted out in theaters and used special costumes and scenery. This is no longer the case— oratorios are performed in concert halls and churches.

Orchestra A mixed group of instruments, including a large number of strings and often wind and percussion as well. The most common type of orchestra is the symphony orchestra, which is made up of four different sections— strings, woodwind, brass, and percussion. There are also other types, such as the chamber orchestra (a small version of the symphony orchestra), string orchestra (string instruments only), and theater orchestra (used in theaters to accompany musicals or ballets).

Organum An early form of polyphonic music based on the melodies used in plainsong, which was first used in the A.D. 800s.

Overture An instrumental composition used to introduce

a dramatic work such as an opera or an oratorio, though sometimes also performed as a concert piece on its own.

Part The music used by each of the different groups of performers in a musical ensemble. For example, in orchestral music, the "cello part" is the name for the music played by the cellos.

Pedal A lever on a musical instrument that is pressed by the foot. Sometimes pedals are used as a way of playing notes (e.g. organ), sustaining them, making them sound quieter (e.g. piano), or changing their pitch (e.g. kettledrum or harp). *Also,* a word used in harmony to describe a note that is held or played repeatedly while the melody and harmonies of the piece change around it.

Phrase A group of notes that make up a section of a melody. "Phrase marks"— curved lines above or below the staff—are sometimes used to show which notes or bars make up each phrase.

Pitch How high or low a musical sound is. Each sound is made up of vibrations. The number of vibrations per second is known as the "frequency." A note that is high in pitch will vibrate more quickly and have a higher frequency than a low-pitched one.

Plainsong A form of vocal music based on the religious texts traditionally used in the Roman Catholic church. The melodies are based around special scales known as "modes," and they are usually sung unaccompanied, either by soloists, or by a choir singing in unison. This form of music is often referred to as Gregorian chant.

Polyphony A word meaning "many sounds," used to describe music that combines at least two independent melodic lines. Another word with a similar meaning is "counterpoint."

Pop music Originally a style of music that appeared during the 1950s in the United States. Today, pop music is a general term used to describe many different kinds of popular, nonclassical music including rock, reggae, dance, and soul. Songs are the most common form of pop music.

Program music Music inspired by literature, art, or nature, and used to tell a story or make the listener imagine pictures or places. The opposite of absolute music.

Punk rock A kind of rock music that combines simple tunes and harmonies with lyrics about rebellion against authority. It became popular in Britain and the United States during the 1970s, through such bands as the Sex Pistols.

Quadruple time Music that has four beats in each bar for example, 4/4 or 12/8.

Quartet The word used to describe a composition for four voices or instruments, or the group of people who perform it. For example, the words "string quartet" can either describe a piece of chamber music written for two violins, viola, and cello, or the four musicians who play this type of piece. There are notable quartets by most of the great composers.

Raga One of the many patterns of notes on which pieces of Indian classical music are based. The notes of each *raga* are specially chosen to conjure up a particular mood or emotion, for example

bravery or love. Different *ragas* are played according to the time of day or season.

Ragtime A type of dance music, usually composed for solo piano, that became popular in the United States in the late 1800s. A rag, or a ragtime piece, was generally in 2/4 or 4/4 time, with a marchlike bass line played by the left hand, while the right hand played a syncopated melody over the top. The most famous piano rags were written by Scott Joplin, composer of the "Maple Leaf Rag" and "The Entertainer."

Rap A kind of pop music that first appeared during the 1970s in New York. In rap music, words are spoken rhythmically rather than being sung to a tune.

Reed A piece of cane or metal that vibrates when air passes across it, used to produce a sound in reed instruments such as the saxophone, accordion, and

Oboe   Clarinet

organ. Apart from the flute, all the woodwind instruments of the orchestra use reeds. Some use one (e.g. clarinet), and some two (e.g. oboe).

Refrain The part of a song that is repeated at the end of each verse or section. In popular music of the 1900s the word "chorus" has the same meaning.

Reggae A kind of popular Jamaican music that first appeared during the 1960s, and since then has influenced pop music around the world. Reggae music is in quadruple time (generally 4/4), with a strong accent on the second and fourth beats of each bar.

Register The range of the human voice is split into paths known as registers. Each one is associated with a different area of the body, and has its own distinctive sound. For example, the low register is sometimes known as the chest voice because low notes seem to resonate in the chest of the singer. The high register is also called the head voice because high notes seem to resonate in the head of the singer, and so on.

Pitch range of the tenor voice

Requiem A mass that is sung in remembrance of people who have died. "Requiem" is a Latin word meaning "rest."

Rest A silence in music, or the sign used to represent it. There are many different types of rest, for example a quarter rest, which lasts for one quarter beat, an eighth rest, which lasts for one eighth beat, and so on.

Rhythm The pattern of long and short notes in a piece of music—also, the number of beats in each bar, the use of accented notes, and so on. Rhythm has nothing to do with tempo. However quickly or slowly a piece is played, the rhythm stays the same. Along with melody and harmony, rhythm is one of the most important elements used in music.

Rock music A type of pop music with strong rhythms and a heavy beat, that was known as "rock'n'roll" when it first became popular in the United States in the 1950s. Rock music is usually performed by groups that include a lead singer, amplified guitars, and drums.

Romantic music Mainly composed between 1830 and 1900, Romantic music was freer and more emotional than the music of the Classical and Baroque periods. Among the forms that became popular at this time were *lieder* and the tone poem (a type of orchestral program music). Many famous operas, symphonies, and concertos were also written in this period, by composers such as Johannes Brahms and Richard Wagner.

Scale A series of notes played one after the other, either from the lowest note to the highest (an ascending scale) or from the highest note to the lowest (a descending scale). There are many different types, for example major, minor, and chromatic scales.

Scale of C major

Scherzo An Italian word meaning "jest" or "joke." A lively and often humorous piece in triple time. Generally the *scherzo* is used as the 2nd or 3rd movement of a work such as a sonata, string quartet, or symphony. Ludwig van Beethoven wrote many memorable *scherzi*.

Score A copy of a piece of music in which all the different instruments' parts are shown. A conductor will use a score to look at all the parts at the same time.

GLOSSARY

Serial music Music composed using a 12-note technique known as serialism. A composer of serial music might not only use a series of notes as the basis for a piece, but also a series of note lengths or dynamics. Sometimes, all the different elements of the music are controlled in this way, for example tone quality attack. This is known as total serialism.

Sforzando An instruction to make a note sound "forced" or emphasized. Another word with the same meaning is *sforzato*. Both words can be shortened to *sf* or *sfz* when they are written on a piece of music.

Sharp A sign that raises the pitch of the note that follows it by a half step. The sign also affects all the other notes of the same pitch that appear later in the same bar. *Also,* a word that describes a musical sound or performance which is higher in pitch than it should be.

Solo A piece (or section of a piece) composed for a single voice or instrument, either with or without accompaniment.

Sonata One of the most important forms of instrumental music from the Baroque period until the present day. A sonata often has three or four contrasting movements, and is generally composed either for a solo instrument, or for one or more other instruments usually with piano accompaniment. For example, a flute sonata is a sonata for flute and piano and so on.

Song A short composition for solo voice, either with or without accompaniment. The song is one of the oldest and most popular musical forms, and features in the musical traditions of all peoples.

Staccato An Italian word that means "detached." Staccato notes (usually shown by a small dot above the head of each one) should be played slightly shorter than usual.

Staff/stave A set of five parallel lines used in musical notation. Notes are placed on and around the lines of the staff, and a clef is added at the beginning to show the exact pitch of each note.

Stop A handle or switch on an organ that is used to control the flow of air into the pipes and, as a result, the sound the organ makes.

Swing A form of jazz that became very popular during the 1930s and 1940s. Swing was often played by "big bands" for example, the bands of Duke Ellington, Count Basie, and Benny Goodman, and people not only enjoyed listening to swing but dancing to it as well.

Symphony One of the most popular and important forms of instrumental music since the Classical period. Symphonies are composed for orchestra, and usually include four contrasting movements, each one with a slightly different mood or tempo. Because the symphony often uses a similar structure to a sonata, it is sometimes described as a kind of "sonata for orchestra."

Syncopation An effect created when an accent is placed on a note that would not normally be accented. Each bar of music is made up of strong and weak beats—for example, in 4/4, beats one and three are stronger than beats two and four. When a note on a weak beat is accented and made to sound more important than a note on a strong beat, the rhythm is said to be syncopated. Syncopation is found in many different types of music, particularly in the rhythms of traditional African music and jazz.

Tempo The speed of a piece of music. Traditionally, composers have used tempo markings to describe the speed of their music, but these only give the performer a rough idea. A more exact way of describing tempo is to use a metronome mark. For example, M.M. ♩ = 60 tells you that the piece should be played at a speed of 60 quarter beats per minute. M.M. ♩ = 100 means there are 100 half beats in a minute. M.M. stands for Maelzels's metronome.

Tempo markings

Adagio	At a leisurely pace, or slow
Allegretto	Quite quick, but not as quick as allegro
Allegro	Quick
Andante	At a walking pace, slower than allegretto, but faster than adagio
Andantino	Sometimes a little slower than andante, but usually means a little quicker
Largo	Slow and dignified
Lento	Slow
Moderato	At a moderate speed, neither fast nor slow
Presto	Very fast
Vivace	Lively

Time signature A sign that appears after the clef and the key signature of a piece of music. It is used to show how many beats there are in each bar and what type of beats they are. For example, 3/4 means that there are three quarter notes in each bar, 4/2 means that there are four half notes in each bar.

Tonal music Music that is based on a major or minor key. Tonal music may modulate (move into a different key) in the middle of a piece, but it is always based on one key at a time. This is unlike bitonal music (which uses two different keys at once), polytonal music (which uses many different keys), and atonal music (which is not based on any key at all).

Tonic The first note (or "keynote") of a scale.

Transcription A piece of music that has been changed in some way; a kind of "arrangement." In a transcription, the original piece may be adapted so that it can be played by different instruments from the ones the composer intended. It may also be simplified to make the music easier for a beginner to play, or it can be made more difficult so that it can be used as a musician's showpiece.

Transposition A technique used to change the pitch of a piece of music. For example, a piece in the key of C major can be "transposed" into D major by raising each of the notes by a half step.

Triad A three-note chord made up of any note, plus the notes a third and a fifth above it. For example, C-E-G (the "common chord" of C major).

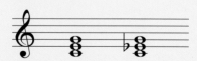

Trio The word used to describe a composition for three voices or instruments, or the group of people who perform it. For example, the words "piano trio" can either describe a piece of chamber music written for piano, violin, and cello, or the group of three musicians who play this kind of piece.

Triplet   A group of three equal notes (or notes and rests), played in the time normally taken by two notes of the same length.

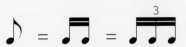

Triple time   Music that has three beats in each bar for example, 3/4 or 9/8.

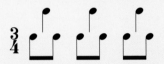

Troubadour   Another word for minstrel. In the strictest sense, however, the troubadour was a wandering musician or poet who lived in southern France during the 1100s or 1200s.

Twelve-note composition
A method of composing music in which all twelve notes of the chromatic scale are of equal importance.

Twelve-note scale   Another name for the chromatic scale.

Unison   A word used to describe notes that are sung or played either at the same pitch, or in octaves. If a choir sings in unison, it means that they are all singing the same tune, though the high voices (sopranos and altos) may be singing an octave higher than the low ones (tenors and basses).

Virtuoso   A performer who has outstanding technical ability.

Voice   The sound produced in humans when air passes over the vocal cords and makes them vibrate. The four most common types of singing voice are bass, tenor, alto, and soprano. *Also,* a word used to describe any of the different parts or melodic lines in a contrapuntal piece such as a fugue.

Voices
   Alto   The highest adult male voice, often used in early forms of vocal music. *Also,* a shortened form of the word "contralto."
   Baritone   An adult male voice with a range higher than a bass but lower than a tenor.
   Bass   The lowest male voice.
   Contralto   The lowest female voice, sometimes also known as an "alto."
   Countertenor   A high adult male voice, most often used in music composed before the end of the 1700s.
   Mezzo-soprano   A word meaning "half soprano," used to describe a female voice that is higher than an alto but lower than a soprano.
   Soprano   The highest female voice. A boy with the same vocal range as a soprano is known as a "treble."
   Tenor   An adult male voice, higher than a baritone or bass but lower than a countertenor or alto.

Waltz   A dance in triple time that originally appeared in Germany and Austria at the end of the 1700s. It soon developed into a graceful ballroom dance and has remained popular ever since.

Index

The publishers would like to thank the following for supplying photographs to this book:

Page 10 Academia Archives *t*; **10/11** Keith Saunders *b*, Zefa *m*; **12** Mary Evans *t*; **12/13** Zefa *b*; **13** Trip *l*, LFI *t*; **14** Adrian de Groot; **15** Ancient Art and Architecture *t*; Travel Photo International *b*; **16/17** Zefa *b*; **17** Trip *r*, Zefa *t*; **18** Werner Forman *t*; **19** Robert Harding Picture Library *r*, Werner Forman *t*; **20** Holford *t*, Robert Harding Picture Library *b*; **20/21** Panos; **21** J. Allen Cash *br*, Zefa *tr*; **22** Trip; **23** Hutchison; **24** Werner Forman *t*; **24/25** Trip *b*; **25** Hutchison *t*; **26** Holford; **26/27** Hutchison; **27** Robert Harding Picture Library; **28** ET Archive *t*, Hutchison *b*; **28/29** Zefa; **29** Hutchison *t*, Ronald Grant Archive *b*; **30** © Horniman *b*, Werner Forman *t*; **30/31** Robert Harding Picture Library; **31** Zefa *b*, Robert Harding Picture Library *t*; **32** Werner Forman; **33** Robert Harding Picture Library; **34** Mary Evans *bl*, ET Archive *br*, Trinity College *t*; **34/35** Holford; **35** Mary Evans *t*; **36** Academia Archives *t*, *br*; **37** The Royal Academy of Music *b*, The Bridgeman Art Library *t*; **38** Zefa *b*, Academia Archive *t*; **39** AKG-London *t*, Reed Consumer Books *b*; **40** Wedgewood Museum *t*, AKG-London *b*; **40/41** Deutsches Theatre museum *b*, *t*; **41** © Larousse *t*; **42** The Bridgeman Art Library *l*, Mansell *b*; **42/43** The Bridgeman Art Library; **43** AKG-London; **44** Academia Archives *t*, Haags Gemeentemuseum *b*; **44/45** Mary Evans *t*, Mansell *b*; **45** Artothek; **46** Mary Evans *t*, AKG-London *b*; **46/47** Image Select; **47** AKG-London *t*, Clive Barda *b*; **48** Camera Press *b*, The Bridgeman Art Library *t*; **49** AKG-London *t*, © Schott, Performing Arts *m*, *b*; **50** Range *t*, *bl*, Aquarius *br*; **51** Redferns *t*, *b*, Bettman *m*; **52** Range *t*, Mander and Michenson *bl*; **52/53** Photofest *b*, *t*; **53** Clive Barda *br*, Zefa *tr*; **54** Range *t*, Hulton-Getty *b*; **54/55** Photofest *b*, *t*; **55** Photofest *m*; **56** Apple Corps *b*, Range *t*; **57** Redferns *l*, Rex Features *t*, LFI *r*; **58** Horniman *m*, *bl*, © Larousse *t*; **59** © Larousse; **60** © Larousse; **61** © Keith Duurders *b*, Yamaha *t*; **62** The Bridgeman Art Library *t*; **63** Zefa *t*, Redferns *m*, Robbie Jack *b*; **64** ET Archive *t*; **65** Performing Arts *br*, © Horniman *t*; **66** The Bridgeman Art Library *t*, © Horniman *b*; **66/67** © Horniman *b*, © Larousse *t*; **67** © Horniman *t*; **68** The Bridgeman Art Library *t*; **69** Hutchison *b*, Rex Features *m*, © Edinburgh *t*; **70** ET Archive *t*, Robert Harding Picture Library *m*; **70/71** © Larousse; **71** Zefa *tl*, Rex Features *tr*, © Larousse *br*; **72** The Bridgeman Art Library *t*; **73** © Larousse *br*, Redferns *t*, Topham Picture Library *m*; **74** Ann Ronan at Image Select *tl*; **75** Robert Harding *tr*, Hutchison *b*, *tl*; **76** Sonia Halliday *t*; **76/77** © Larousse; **77** Performing Arts *t*, Camera Press *b*; **78** © Larousse *r*, Sonia Halliday *t*, Range *l*; **79** Hutchison *t*, © Larousse *l*; **80** ET Archive *t*, © Horniman *b*; **81** © Laroussse *l*, © Horniman *b*, Robbie Jack *r*; **82** Sonia Halliday *t*, © Horniman *b*; **83** © Larousse *t*, Rex Features *b*; **84** Mary Evans *t*, © Larousse *m*; **84/85** © Larousse; **85** Pica Press Foto *b*, © Larousse *m*; **86** ET Archive *t*, Harrison and Harrison *b*; **87** Keith Saunders *b*, Performing Arts *tr*, Victoria and Albert *tl*; **88** Lebrecht Collection *t*; **88/89** Yamaha; **89** Robert Harding Picture Library *b*, Aquarius *tr*, Redferns *m*; **90** ET Archive; **91** Zefa *b*, ET Archive *t*, *b*; **92** © Larousse *t*, J. Allan Cash *b*; **93** Panos *tr*, Image Select *tl*; **94** Werner Forman *t*, Hutchison *t*; **95** Hutchison *t*, *b*, Magnum *br*; **96** Ancient Art and Architecture *t*, Pressens Bild *b*; **97** Hutchison *t*, Random Dance Company *r*; **98** AKG-London *t*, LFI *b*; **98/99** Redferns; **99** Performing Arts *tr*, Aquarius *tl*; **100** Hutchison *r*, Lenn Hardy of Matthew Brady *t*; **101** © Larousse *b*, Rex Features *t*; **104** AKG-London *tl*, Image Select *bl*, © Larousse *r*; **105** AKG-London *t*, Clive Barda *b*; **106** Aquarius *mr*, National Portrait Gallery *ml*, Image Select *b*; **107** AKG-London *t*, © Larousse *r*; **108** © Larousse *l*; **108/9** © Larousse *t*, Hulton-Getty *b*; **109** Hulton-Getty *t*, © Larousse *r*; **111** Mary Evans *br*; **118** © Larousse; **120** © Larousse; **121** © Larousse; **122** © Larousse; **123** © Larousse; **124** © Larousse; **125** © Larousse.

Artists

Harry Chow, Eugene Fleury, Chris Forsey, Pamela Goodchild (B. L. Kearley), Mike Lacey (Simon Girling Assoc.), Patrick Mulrey, Roy Flooks, Darren Paterson (Garden Studio), Clive Spong (Linden Artists), Catherine Ward (Simon Girling Assoc.)

The publishers would also like to thank the following for their contribution to this book:

Claire Berridge, Margaret Birley, Boosey and Hawkes, Quentin Daniel, Katie Elliot, Embassy of Indonesia, Roy Flooks, Kelly Flynn, General Boffin Media, Eddie Grabham, Nina Hathaway, Honor Head, Paul Lawley, Julia March, Mel Pickering, Premiere, Mike Sheppard and Music Sales, Professor Denis Stevens, Peter Thoms, Victor Stevenson, Dave Whitehead, The Witch Ball, Yamaha, Eleanor Van Zandt.